Why Drawing Naked Women

is good for the soul

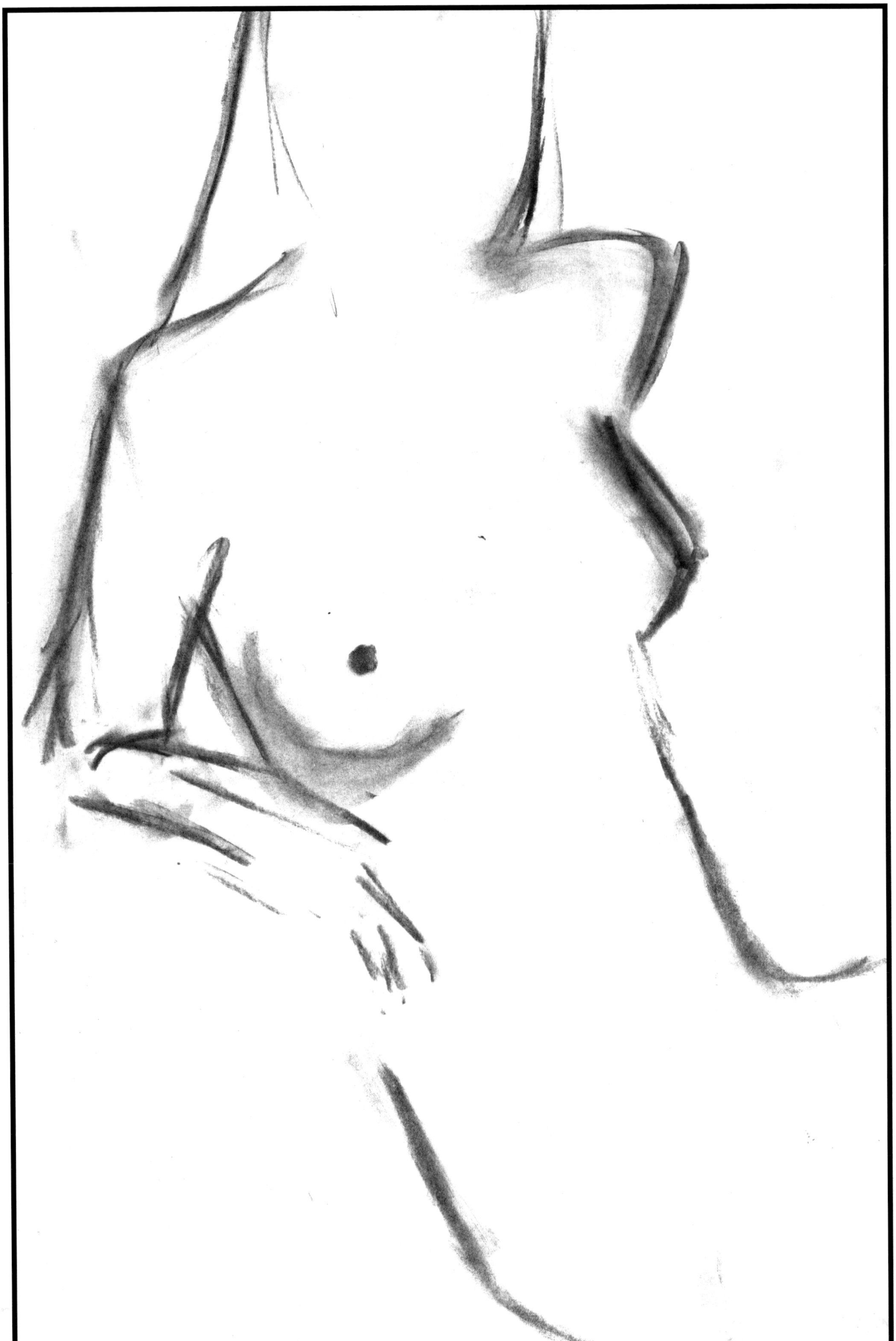

Why Drawing Naked Women

is good for the soul

John Bird

The Word Machine

First published 2013.

The Word Machine CIC.

www.thewordmachine.org

ISBN: 978 0 9576 2941 7

9 8 7 6 5 4 3 2 1

A catalogue reference for this book is available from the British Library.

Printed by CMC London.
www.contentmc.co.uk

Notting Hill, London. 2013.

They projected onto the big back screens enormous pictures of naked women. Fronts, backs, undercarriages; laying down, standing up, crouching, sleeping. All the drawings were mine. The crowded audience looked at this vast presentation of small drawings projected big with as much awe as I did. I had not seen this enlarging of small drawings before. The talk organizer had not told me there would be this kind of backdrop to my talk.

The man sitting in front of me smiled over his clipboard. The audience of perhaps 400 talked among themselves, seemingly overwhelmed by the powerful graphic images of female nakedness. I was overwhelmed. A quick gesture with a pencil, magnified into a giant gesture over thirty foot high, seemed odd. Like giant gestures on giant pieces of paper.

Silence fell and the man began his questioning.

'So. You draw. As we can see here. And as your book graphically tells us.'

'I draw. But never at this scale and size. I do some small works. You have taken some of them here and made them into something which they were never intended to be. I don't draw at thirty foot heights.'

'We wanted to create a sense of the largeness of drawing in your life. You suggest that drawing civilised you and overwhelmed your bad side. And we wanted that feeling to be captured in this talk this evening.'

I would not argue. There was some strange logic to it. I was claiming that drawing naked women took me from an obliterated, criminal life, an underclass life, into something different.

'Explain the first occasion that you took up a pencil.'

'Probably when I was a child. As we all do. We draw like Picasso until we are about 11. And then we start drawing, most of us anyway, as if our creativity has been amputated. That is the weird thing about drawing and painting and all the other creative things we do.'

A few months before the talk I had been on a beach in Northern France, walking over dunes towards the sea. I came over a large dune on this deserted beach and saw an embarrassing sight. A woman was crouching down urinating and the moment I saw her, she saw me. She jumped up and I shouted, 'Excuse me.' I turned to walk another way. But the gorse was so thick on either said of me I could only turn and walk back to where I had come from. She shouted after me. 'Monsieur, please.' So I stopped and turned and was at a loss as to what to do. She came up to me. I felt like the biggest fool in the world. I had wandered off the accepted path from the campsite I was staying in into the gorse and the patches of sand. I was going to conquer my lack of regard for drawing water and I carried one of my bigger sketchbooks.

She came up and laughed nervously.

'Sir, we were both caught by that.'

The path led directly to a tent that was pitched within the gorse and sand. It was almost hidden. A place where you could forget about the world; until of course you wanted to piss.

'I really am sorry. I am in the campsite there and I was on the way to the sea to draw some sun and sea and sand.'

'Look. I am the one. I take up a private place in a public place. I am the culprit.'

Her English was good.

'I will simply retrace my steps.'

She would not have it.

'No, if you go by the bush there, and then go to your left, then right, for maybe 200 metres you will get your sea.'

She was in her early twenties. She smiled and was dark haired and strong faced. The wind whipped her hair around. She had a broad smile and she seemed now to have regained her composure. She was beautiful.

'Thank you. If you ever want to use the smallest room I would go into the campsite. There are good facilities.'

'I must remember. Thank you.'

I smiled and touched my imaginary cap, as many men did in embarrassment.

'Have a good hide out.'

'I was just going to make some coffee, sir. I have some croissants I got from the village. Would you join me? And show me your sketchbook?'

I looked at the woman and imagined myself drawing her. Her, laying quietly, and occasionally telling me what was motivating the mood or feeling or situation she was in. Little did I know that I would spend the next week drawing her almost daily in her sand tent. And out of that would come the best collection of drawings I had committed since my young manhood; when back then I devoted the time and energy to one thing and one thing alone: drawing.

'Yes. Thank you. I was going to a café. Why not sit and talk for a few minutes.'

I sat on a small stool and she prepared the coffee. And then when we sat over the coffee she told me about her life. A student. At the Sorbonne. Studying philosophy. And then we fell to looking at my drawings. Most of the drawings were of women. Some of men, many also of trees and plants. But mainly they were the work of the female body. And she looked at them with great interest.

'You must draw me.'

How many times had I been asked to draw someone? How many times had I asked? Celestine had been the most recent.

'This afternoon? I really must draw the sea. It's necessary.'

'I study. I read. That's all I do. You come when you are ready. But I sleep also. I may sleep while you draw.'

I went down to the beach and drew some light waves and birds, and sand. And clouds and distant boats. The clouds were particularly good out over the English Channel; La Manche, the Sleeve as the French call it. I tried hard to bring some depths to my clouds, but I was asking the impossible of myself. Then sitting carefully on the back of an abandoned chair I drew waves again and again. And began to realise, as with drawing leaves, each little bit of the drawing has to get a personality. After a few hours I think I had learned more about water and clouds than I had all of my time as a drawer. Which stretched back over four decades.

I came back up the slope of thick sand, soft underfoot. As I approached the gorse and knew the tent would

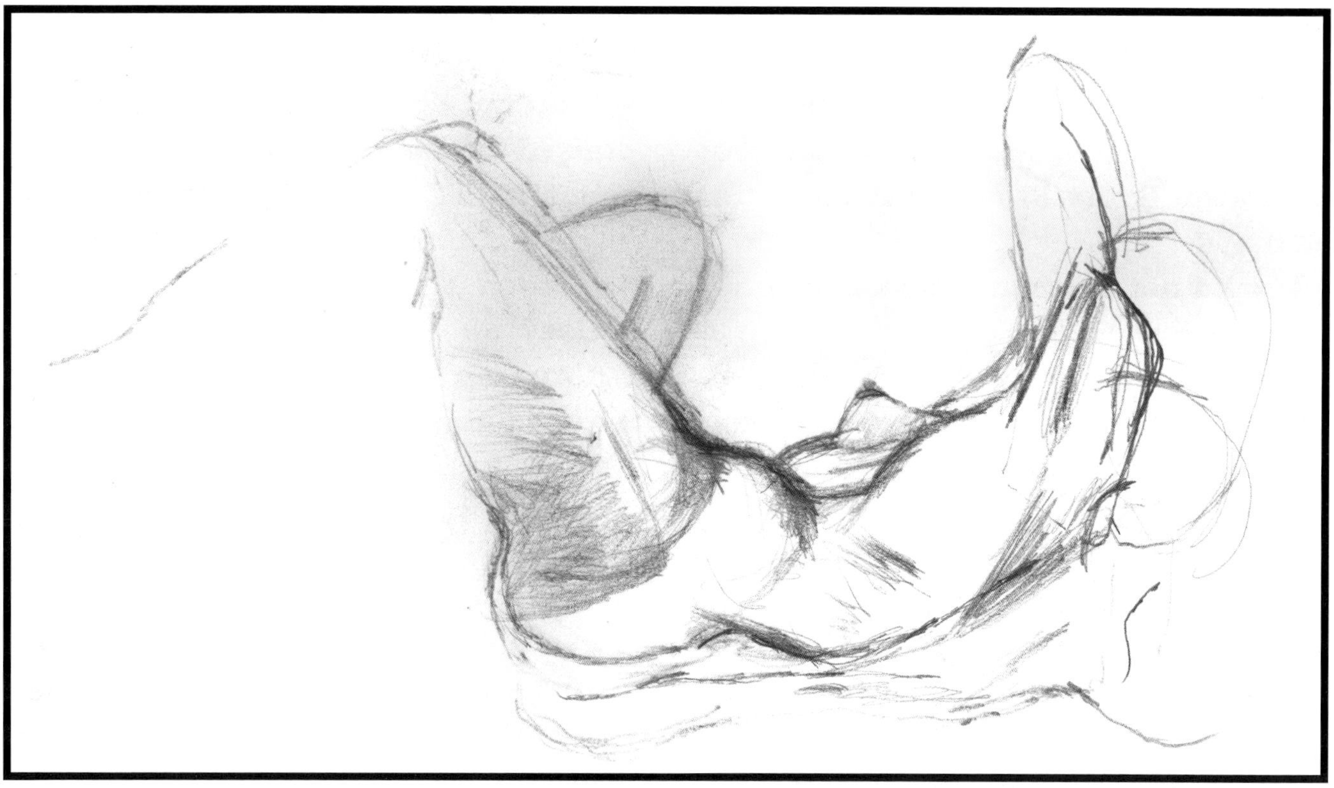

be over the next sand-duned ridge, I began to feel awkward. Our sudden rapport had been based so flimsily on her being caught out squatting. Such thin things bring people together. Yet there was out in the world, I knew, people so open to new things. And I was a new thing.

At the next ridge I could not see her about. I walked up close to the tent and she was laying there with glasses on, asleep with a book on her breasts. She looked full of what knowledge can do to someone, if used well. So at peace with the world. I pulled up one of her small stools and almost squatting down, began to draw her. She stirred once or twice, and Jean Paul Sartre slipped out of her hands. But I was drawing her face and hair mostly. Drawing sleeping people is something different. People have to feel happy with you as they sleep. Once I was drawn by a girlfriend asleep and it was a very different drawing to my animated face. Now I drew Delphine, unanimated.

I drew for half an hour before she stirred, and then looked up in wonder at me drawing her. And smiled.

'You caught me.'

'Sleeping and studying; you seem to do them well.'

'I do. It is also a time of forgetting. Would you like to draw me more?'

'I am already there.'

'But more? More of me?'

'Of course. I want to draw you until either you leave or I leave.'

'Then we must begin.'

She stood and undid her denims, exposing a delicate pair of knickers. White and with some decoration of a filigreed kind. I tried to avoid my eyes. You normally drew naked models when they were completely undressed, arriving wrapped in a bath robe. But Delphine was unwrapping herself before, exposing tanned skin that complimented her light black hair. She pulled down her knickers with such confidence I had to ask,

'Have you been drawn many times before?'

'Never. But I have always wanted to be drawn. Every French girl wants to be drawn.'

I could not agree or disagree, having drawn a few of them.

'It is because we are all romantics. We are stuck in the life of Paris when Picasso drew and Modigliani drew. All French women need to be reassured that they would be drawn by the great men.'

'As a philosopher you should not say such unproveable generalisations.'

'Exactly.'

She said this as if she had just proved a hypothesis. I had to smile. Now, as she stood with her top off and undoing the white, light filigreed bra. Her total body, strong and tanned, with more white where she had covered up with summer bikini. Her strong breasts came bursting out and she stood now complete.

'This is good. Later shall we swim in the sea?'

'Why not?'

As she stood I sketched her quickly. I came up close to her and drew her above me and in front of me. Her neatly trimmed pubic hair was little more than a line that did not manage to cover her lips. I drew on and soon had a few strong drawings. Then Delphine sat and carried on reading.

'I will write about this. This is what happens only in a movie.'

'French, or American?'

'French of course. A lost girl who wants to hide from life and study, is discovered by a wandering drawer. And they draw from then on. Their friendship blossoms because of the pencil.'

I drew. She read. I occasionally praised her concentration. She talked about philosophy and I talked about anything that came into my head. And then I told her the story, over coffee, of the various times that led to my taking up drawing. She listened intently.

'Drawing was good for your soul.'

'I am a devote ex catholic. I lost all that soul stuff.'

'A soul can be as broad as you wish it. Or as narrow as you wish it. It is all the unresolved things about your life that do not fit into your brain or your heart.'

She came back to the mobile home I had rented on the campsite and took a shower. She was tall and good-bodied, with good breasts. And she got me thinking about how I was rescued by drawing. And all the other parts of me were tacked on to that central thing: drawing. And drawing naked women in particular.

'I could not tell you how many naked women I have drawn. Hundreds. Hundreds.'

'You must write about it.'

'I will.'

A few weeks afterward she wrote to me from Paris; now back at the university she wrote: 'Capture those stories you told me on the beach. I think I will never rise above that short time. When the sand and the wind, and the rain and the sun inspired us to work together.'

I wrote back and said that she was a tonic. That I had gone to France to the campsite to get away from the pressures of life, just to draw. And

she had made all of this possible. And that now she was enshrined in many drawings and I would send her some. And she must come to London and be drawn again.

'Drawing is a kind of education, a socialisation for you. You use drawing as a means of perfecting other social skills. Is that what you mean?'

'Art made me want other things out of life, away from crime and wrong doing. It turned me into someone who cared about people.'

The lights were too bright. The images were too strong. There was nothing comfortable about sitting on a stage with the glare and the projections and the whirl of machines. I drank water. The questions seemed inane. I wanted to be away from the heat and the inane questions.

'I am particularly interested in why it is young women, or women in particular, who you have concentrated on, to draw. Why not other things?'

'Women are not things.' He nodded. 'Women, all sizes, and shapes, big or thin: I draw them because I love drawing women.'

He kind of half laughed.

'I was trying to get to the bottom of why you drew women almost exclusively. What is it about women? For as you have said on occasions, it's not just about getting women naked.'

'I draw women because I am fascinated by their bodies. Their beings. When you draw a woman you are drawing all of nature. You are looking at being.'

Every explanation of why you draw naked women will sound trite. I accepted that you could not find an explanation other than you liked doing it. He crossed his legs and then uncrossed them. He had a smirk on his face. He looked at his clipboard. What he was trying to ascertain was: was I simply a man who wanted women to 'get their kit off?' In other words, a sexualised observer who relished nakedness of the opposite sex.

'But, if women are your exclusive preserve...'

'I am interested in women. Women have changed me. It's as simple as that. I look at them and I see the possibility of making some image out of them. Are you suggesting that I am only drawing women because I get some prurient pleasure?'

He leant back in his chair. He was at a loss. I thought I had better help him.

'I was a fucking arsehole. I come from abject poverty. I was a ponce, an arsehole. But I rose above it. And became useful in the world. I used art to get out of the quagmire of my life. Now I am useful in the world. And I owe it all to women, and to art.'

We then fell to talking about politics. I did my best to explain how once I was a vicious little racist and grew out of that. And that art was one of the things that enabled that transformation. The lights blared. The motors moaned, and the questions seemed irrelevant. An hour of this lay ahead of me. I looked about the audience. I had loved the idea of spending an hour and a half talking about art. Now I could not wait to get it over with.

I explained once again that art was useful to me. And that it had proved the great turn in my life. And that drawing naked women was good for my soul.

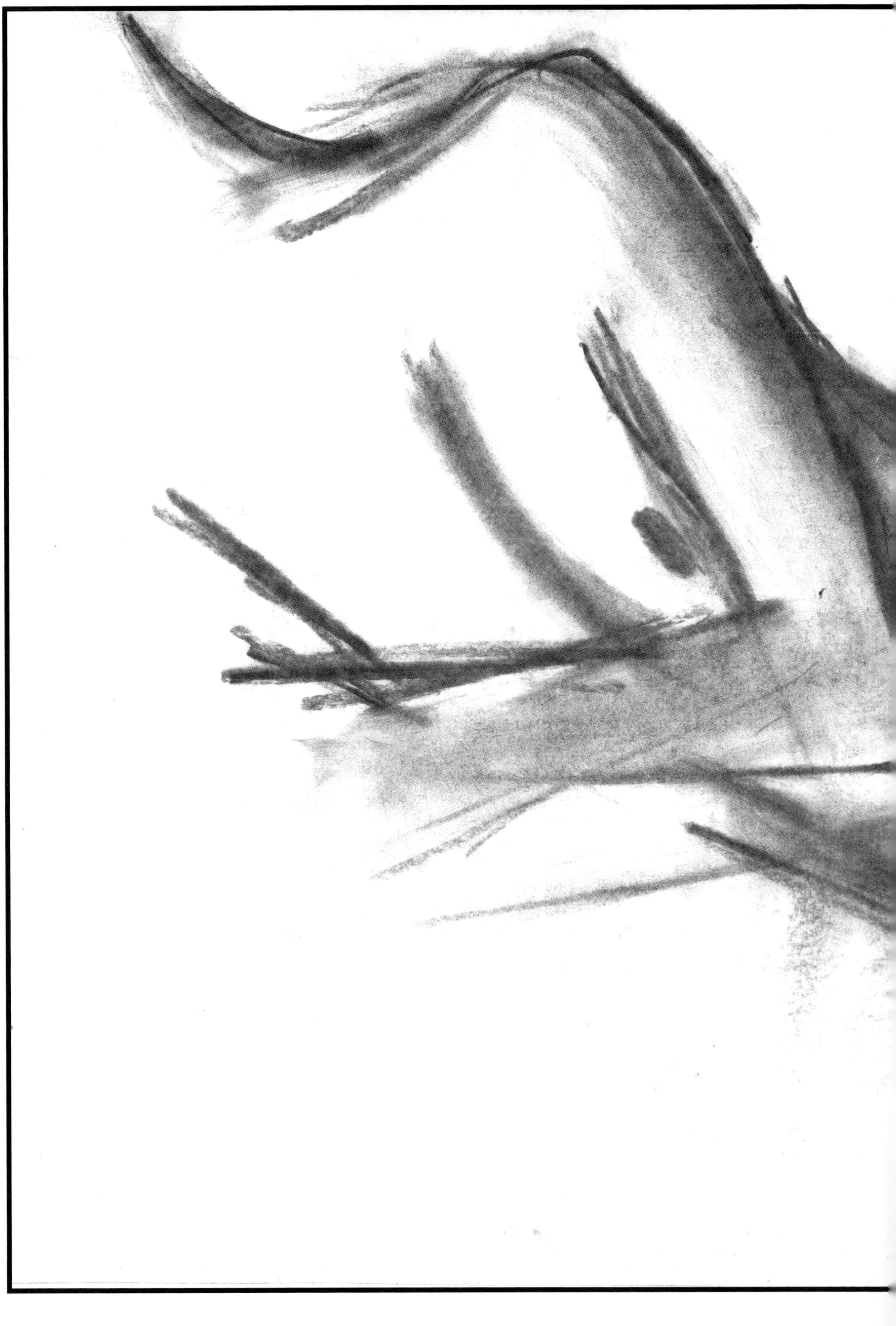

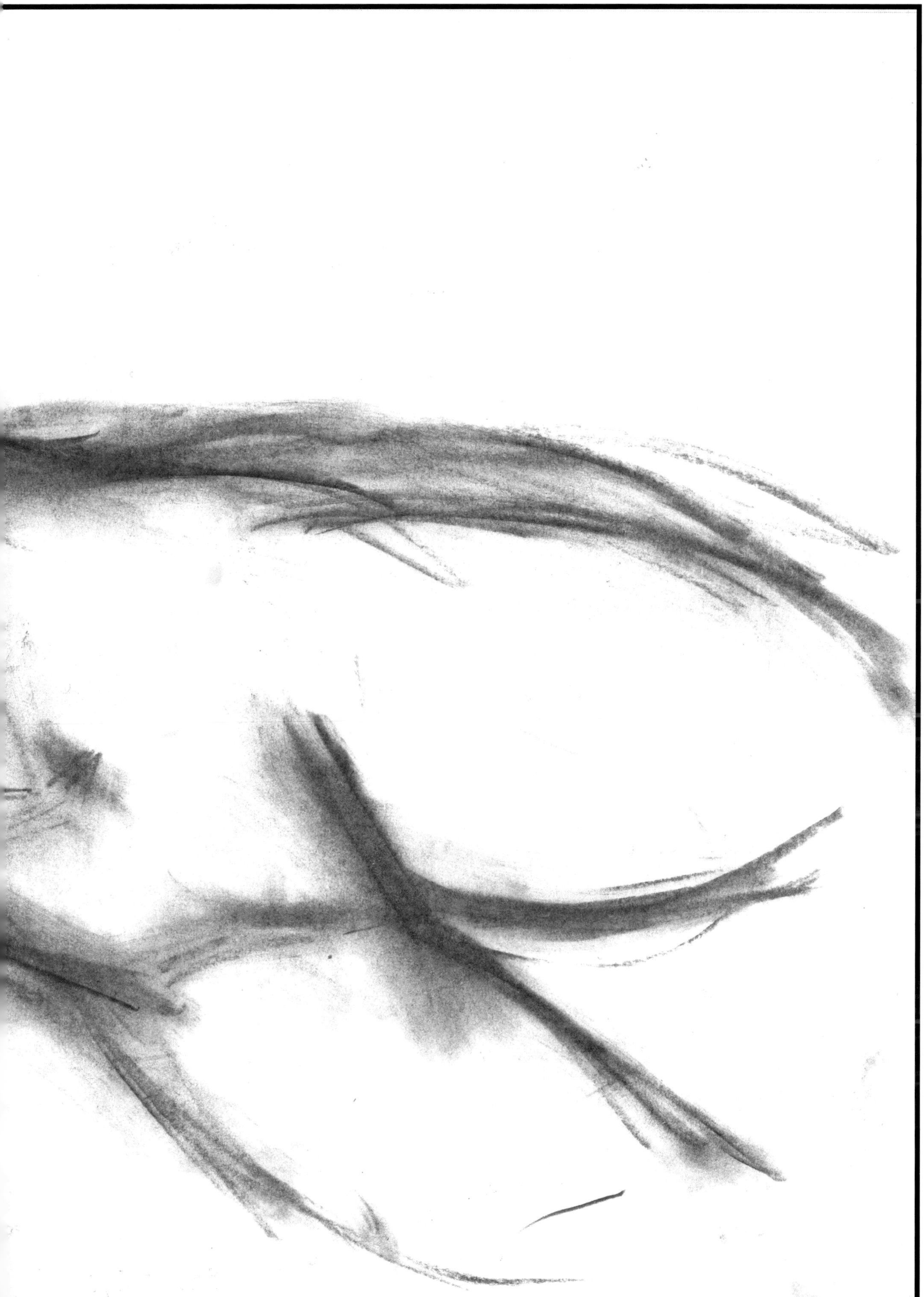

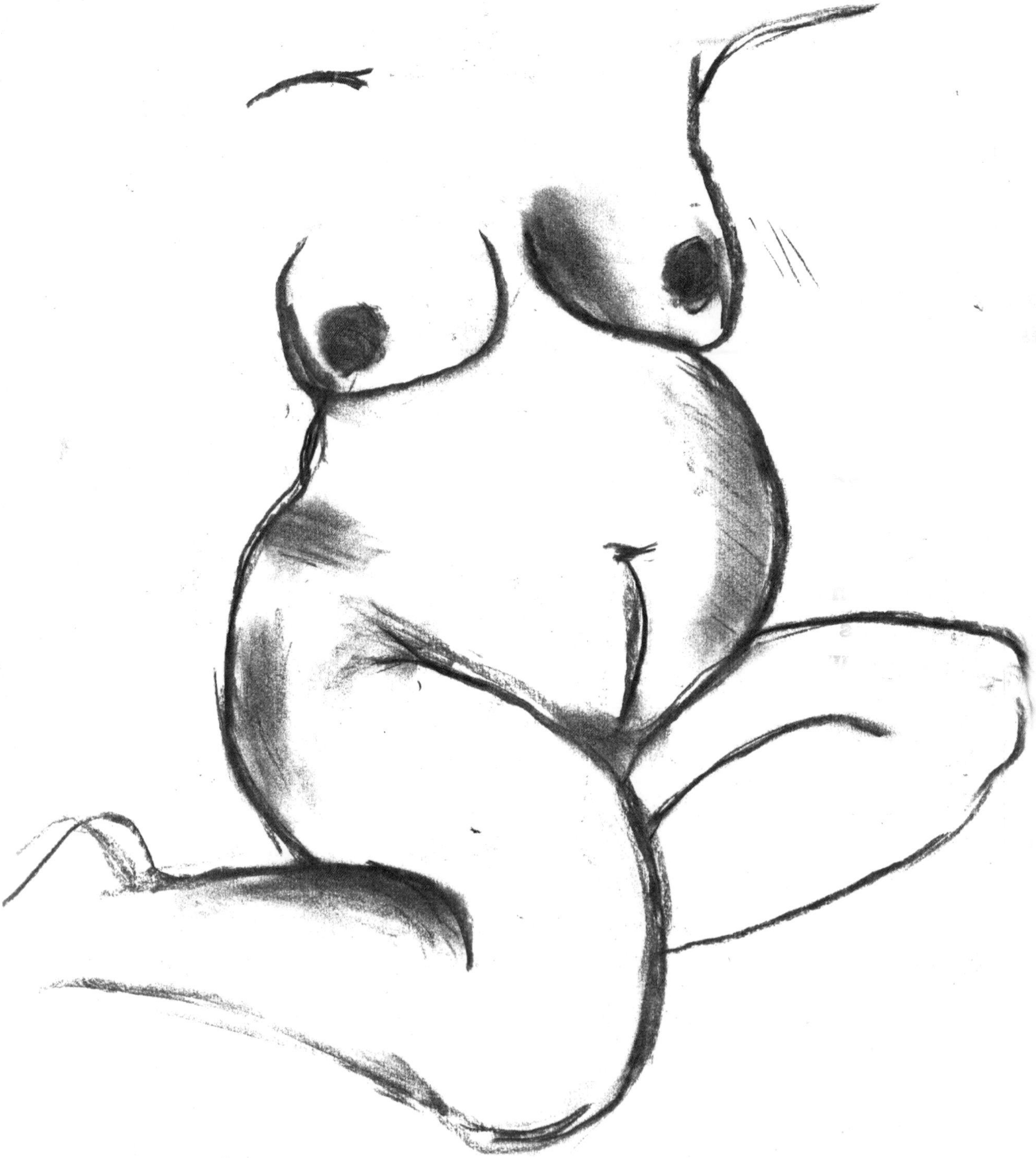

Knightsbridge, London, 1961.

One summer's day a few years before Churchill died, I delivered some wine to a house a few doors from his London house. I rang the bell and from above I heard a man shout: 'Tradesmen's entrance.'

He left the window and a few minutes later popped up from the basement.

'Oi! Down here.'

I followed him down the steps to the area. He held the door open and ushered me in. He had a nasty look on his face. Delivery boys get nasty faces from adults. Adults forgot it was not the 1930s. Adult arseholes talked to you as if they were the master class and you the underclass, because you were 15. They had lived through the war and shot Germans and killed Japanese. And maybe fucked women in potato sheds and threw grenades at the enemy. We had Elvis Presley, and Paul Anka, Gene Vincent, Buddy Holly; we had films and records and we could be our own selves. But when you went to work you realised that they thought you were shit.

'What gives you the effing right to knock on the effing front door? Eh?'

'Where's the notice for tradesmen's?'

'We don't have a notice. We are a cut above. Churchill lives a few doors from us.'

I laughed. I could not help it. This small scrawny man who may have been a hangman in the army had the look of a man who felt he was important.

'You can't be that 'cut above'. My guvnor says you haven't paid for your drinks for almost a year. And if you don't pay this week it's the company's solicitors after yer.'

He kicked the chair. The chair fell over. He snarled.

'Your boss told you the private matters of my employer? A piece of shit like you?'

I was enjoying this.

'And lots more. He said your guvnor did have money but he spunked it away on drink and boys' arses.'

He kicked the chair again, and threw the now empty box on the floor.

'Your boss said all this? It's effing libel. Effing libel.'

I shook my head.

'You don't understand mister. It's libel if it's printed. It's slander if it's said.'

He kicked the box and backed me out towards the door.

'Get out, you piece of rubbish. Get out.'

A door opened and a man with makeup and wild dyed red hair came in. He was wearing a furred dressing gown. His nails had paint on them. He had a cross face.

'What is this shouting for Haliburton? Oh, I see some drink relief.'

And then looking a me.

'And a charming Trollope of a boy to deliver it.'

He smiled and came towards me. His man Haliburton looked down in a shamed way.

'So thank you, you sweet boy, for bringing all of this to me so early in the morning.'

'It's my job Mister. Delivery they call it. For the working classes to do.'

He tittered.

'Oh, not so much of the class stuff

here laddie. We don't recognise the class stuff here. Do we Haliburton?'

'No sir.'

He said this without looking up. I could not avoid a smirk. The master was a complete cunt.

'Would you take a little drink with me boy?'

He said this coming up very close. He smelt of drink and lavender oil.

'No sir. It's illegal to ply drinks on a minor sir. And as a member of the working class I've got to keep working.'

He was put off by this.

'Truculent as well. Ugh! All this class stuff. I bet you've been locked up. You have that kind of bitter face.'

'Not often Mister. Maybe three times.'

The man turned to Haliburton. To scold him.

'We are obviously using the wrong wine merchants Haliburton! How did this happen?'

'We deliver to the Royal family Mister. And you won't be getting any more of the wine and spirits from us. Unless you pay your bills.'

The servant now pushed me towards the door. Though small he was very strong. His master shouted at me.

'Go and tell your company that their services will no longer be required.'

'I'll tell Mister Lindsay Mister. And I'll say you are a straight up and down gentleman. Not the kind who'd piss his money up the wall on booze and boys.'

The servant took a swing at me that missed. I punched him hard on the nose and it bled. He pulled back and slammed the door. I knocked on the door.

'Can I have my cardboard box back mister?'

I cycled off on the bike, passing a house with a policeman standing outside. I stopped and called over to the policeman. 'Is this Churchill's house guvnor?' The policeman shouted back: 'Sir Winston Churchill to you.' I scoffed. 'I bet there ain't one law in this land that says you've got to call Churchill Sir Winston Churchill.' The policemen walked over and took hold of my jacket. 'Would you like me to get you done for Sus, son? Eh? You look as if you've seen the inside of a cell before. And a Black Maria.' I looked at him and said, 'I ain't got no power guvnor. You can say what you like. The world's yours.' He let go of my jacket, pushing me at the same time. I cycled off, but stopped fifty yards away. I looked back at the cunt. I took my fingers and made them shaped like a hand gun. Then I put them to my head and went 'Bang'. And then I cycled off as fast as I could. That really was a cuntish thing to be doing in 1961, before the Liberals took over and watered down the power of coppers. Fortunately the trades bike didn't have a company name on the side. So as long as I got away there was little chance of apprehension. But you could never tell. I was not wanted by the police at the time. But it was easy to get done. 'Sus', Suspicious behaviour, could get you done as easily as if you put a brick through an antique shop window.

I got to the corner near Kensington Gardens and belted down the road, and turned off as soon as I could. Making my way through back streets to Knightsbridge, I was soon back

at the shop. Maude was in the shop bending over some boxes. As I passed I ran my hand over her arse. She did not even spring up. I kept my hand active and explored her undercarriage. When she straightened up she had a red face and was smiling. 'You dirty boy. If my fiancé saw you Tony Bird, he'd chop your dick off and make you swallow it.' I ran my hand over her tits. They were enormous, maybe too big for her good neat body.

'But we know, don't we Maude love, that I can get you wet just looking at you.'

She smiled.

'You teaser. You dirty little muff teaser.'

I squeezed her nipples.

'Next time he's giving you one over the bed with your arse in the air imagine it's me.'

She came forward and gave me a light kiss on the lips, and then pulled back.

'There's a devil in you, Tony Bird. There's no Jesus in you.'

The bell from the basement went. Maude went back behind the counter. I went down to Mister Lindsay. He sat in his office with the little fire on. And the bottle of Dry Old Sack. And a small glass. As I walked in he looked up. 'Can you get me a bacon sandwich, my dear?'

'Yes sir.'

And he gave me the money.

'And have one yourself. Then come and tell me what The Marquess of Queens had to say.'

I went out down Beauchamp Place on the bike and went to a café by Chelsea Juvenile Court. I hoped never

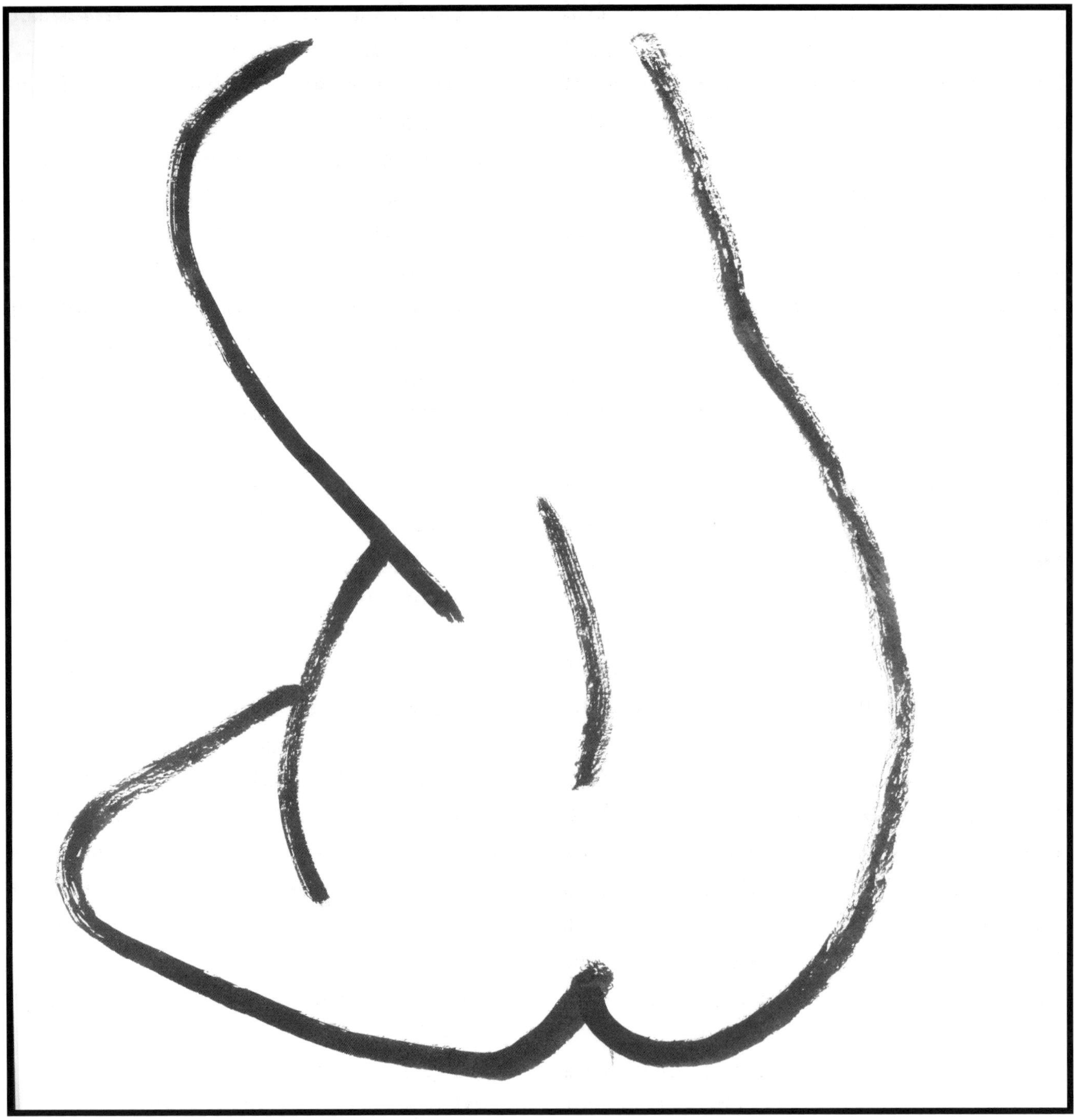

to be charged there again. But I could not entirely trust myself not to get into even more trouble. The world was obviously against me. And I was against the world.

After the bacon sandwich and a chat about the Marquess, as he called him, I loaded up the bike and went off to South Kensington. I saw Tony C on a butcher's bike. He stopped me and looked at the box of drinks I had loaded. 'Any chance of some stuff?'

'There's about ten bottles of Old Grandad that have dust all over them in the cellar. It's a whiskey.'

Tony took out a wad of notes. He gave me £3. 'See what you can get me for that.'

'The next time I'm out I'll take out the ten bottles and leave them with you. In a string bag.'

'No, bring one bottle a night down the World's End. Not ten at a time.'

He cycled off. Tony C had something about money. As if it made no sense, had no meaning. I carried on and ended up in a mews behind Old Brompton Road. I passed a shop I had been sacked from for suspicion of pilfering, and then went into the mews behind it. I rang on the bell door and a very drunk man out. He was splattered with paint and he seemed barely able to stand up. He stood aside and I went in and walked up the stairs. There were paintings all over the place. Splashes and figures. It looked like tripe. Everywhere was paint. Only an old arm chair and a table stood. I put the box on the table and counted out the drinks so that he could see them. And he looked at the order. And staggered and fell into the chair. He asked me to pour him some whiskey. I did it out of a bottle of Cutty Sark. Then he drank it and said, 'Shut the door on the way out.'

Out in the mews I got back on the bike and wondered if the painter had any money. Because he was so drunk you could have taken stuff from him and he would never have known. But I had already shut the door when the thought had occurred to me, so there was no chance to go back in.

I cycled past the shop I had been sacked from, even if they had no proof. I wanted to smash the windows. I hated them for what they had done to me. I looked into the window to see if there was anyone from a few months before who had been there. There were a few new staff. I cycled back to the shop.

At lunch time I took the bike and cycled to the Victoria and Albert museum. I walked down the back, passed the public canteen and up stairs to the Constable drawings and paintings. It was empty except for the guard. I sat on a bench and looked at some of his drawings. I went right up to a few and looked carefully at how Constable drew trees. Each leaf like another, but supposed to be a different leaf. I moved on and looked at big oil sketches he made for big paintings. And wondered, what would it be like to wake up in the morning and after breakfast go into a studio room and paint all day? Paint flowers, women, paint whatever you wanted to paint.

I had to be careful. Often I would be late for returning. Mister Lindsay never said a thing. But I felt he might hate me for taking the piss out of him.

I had a roll in the canteen. I sat with my roll and tea and looked at a big group of girls, probably my age, from some posh school. With all their giggling and looking at me and laughing. Knowing that each of us would have liked to have seen the other naked. I got up and cycled back to the shop. Maude was coming up from downstairs.

'You've been sneaking off for a piss again.'

'A girl needs to.'

'Did you wash your hands?'

She hit me lightly and laughed.

'You must be the funniest boy in the world, Tony Bird.'

As she passed me I squeezed her arse. She stopped.

'You might as well take your handful. I'll be married soon. Then I'll be leaving.'

'Maude, just because your married doesn't mean...'

But the bell went and I went down and discussed with Mister Lindsay the orders and jobs for the afternoon. He

told me that the Marquess of Queens had been on the phone and a cheque would be forthcoming but they did not want ruffian boys delivering. So they would have to go to another company for their business. Mister Lindsay said he wished them the best and suggested Berry Brothers and Rudd, or Stowells of Chelsea. But that a quick expediting of their bill would save embarrassment. I asked Mister Lindsay to explain the word 'Expedite'. He told me and then fell into telling me all sorts of other words that had fallen out of use and needed to be refurbished and dusted down for modern use.

I went out on the bike to South Kensington again and hoped Maude did not leave too soon. That night I went to the night class at Park Walk, having dropped a bottle of Old Grandad off to Tony C. At the night class I tried to draw an imaginary picture of Maude, with her vast tits, overhanging her trim waist. The woman who ran the class came up and looked at me. 'Isn't there some physical imbalance there, Tony?'

She liked me. She liked the fact that I came to her class regularly.

'She works with me, Miss. You can't walk past her without bumping into her knockers.'

'Knockers? That's a new one on me.'

'I prefer it to 'tits', Miss.'

'Whatever. She certainly has some structural problems there. Back problems in her middle age, no doubt.'

I carried on with the drawing. Lilly breezed in, looked around, and then breezed out. She loved art, but she did not want to put the work in. I carried on. I went to the clay tank and began making a model of Maude, her back, her arse and her tits. But the tits sagged and I could see what the art teacher meant. Poor Maude's back was probably working overtime supporting her tits. But when she got older she'd need more than the usual bra. She might need some scaffolding.

After the night class I went for a drink with the boys and we talked about work. And girls. But we didn't talk about art. Art was not for them. After a few drinks I went home. My mum was waiting saying, as she always said,

'When you're working you have to be home early.'

I went to bed thinking of Maude and her super tits and hoping that one day I might draw them. And slept in the shadows of the gas works and the hooting sounds of the river.

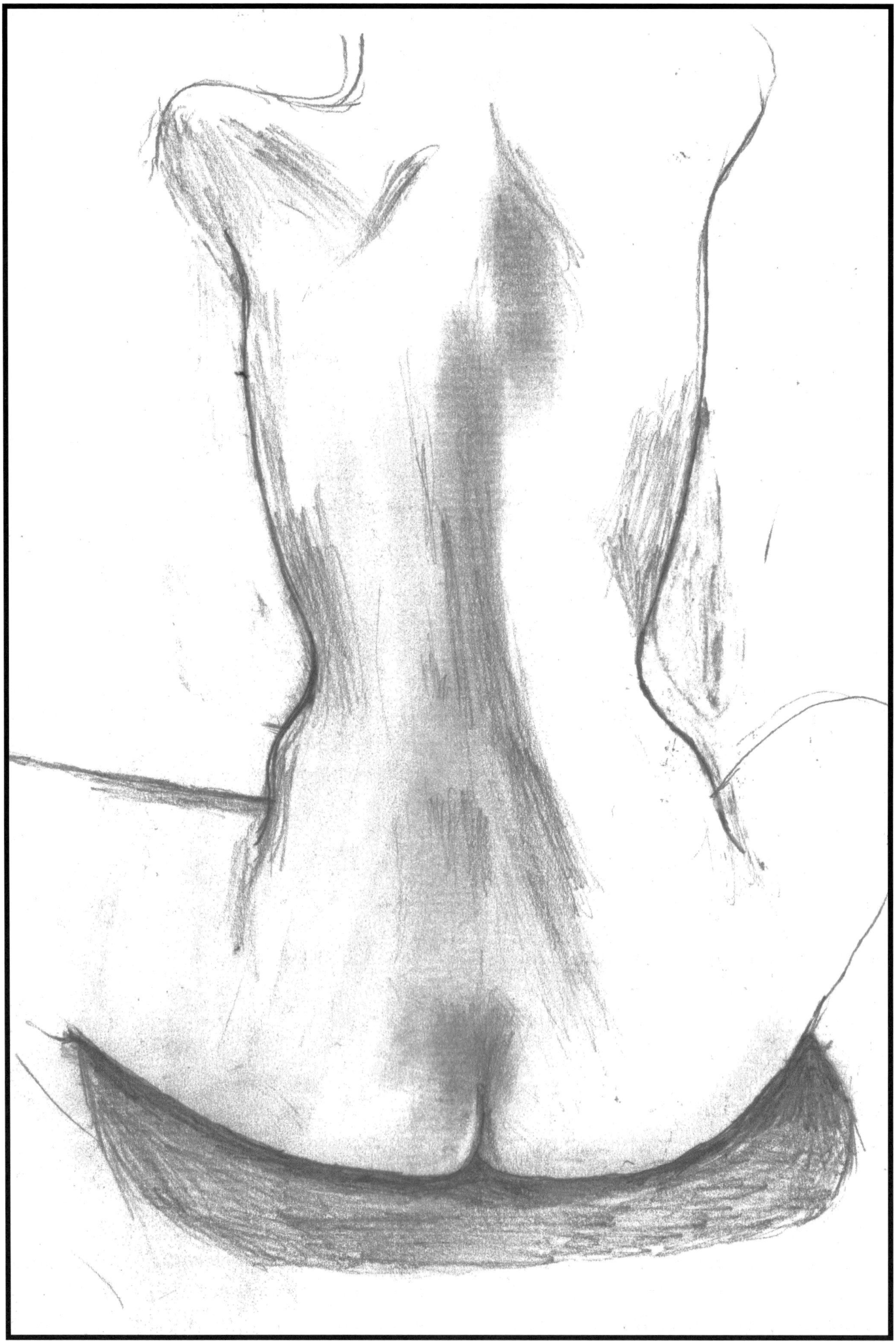

King's Road, Chelsea. 1961.

When I dropped the girl in the fire that night and burnt her clothes and lightly scorched her arse, I was about a hundred miles from home. That put the kibosh on me staying. The next morning I hitched to London from the little place in the country. I got to the King's Road Chelsea at about 11pm. I was tired, hungry and dirty. I walked down Blacklands Terrace and a girl a few years older than my fifteen years stood looking in the window of the John Sandoe Bookshop. The light was poor but I could tell even in the limited light that she was a middle class stunner. Her arse was strong. Her tits of a good size. Her face soft and beautiful. And her hair was a golden red blonde. She turned as I approached and managed a smile. I made my play:

'Excuse me Miss, any chance of a shilling or two to get a Wimpy burger up at Earls Court? They're open all night. Well, until 6am when they close for half an hour for cleaning.'

She turned and looked at me. She spent a few seconds touring my face with her eyes. I could tell she was assessing me. A slight smile played around her full red lips.

'God boy. You look like a washed-out boy Lord Byron.'

'Maybe Miss. A hungry one.'

She looked even more, as if she was enjoying this.

'Tell me a poem.'

'A poem?'

'A poem. That's the key.'

'The key to what?'

'The key to the next good thing.'

I cleared my throat for my recital. I would tell the one I composed down by the Serpentine the last summer. Before all the stuff went wrong:

'Oh Sick sick man, what has thou done? For the battle was not won. People stare with squint eyes, for they too realise that loose of mind brings Goodbyes. Lay down your weapon, lay it down and repent. People watch, they know your bent. So, gather forth little creatures and man will pour forth his wonderful adventures.'

She was moved.

'You made that up?'

'Down by the Serpentine in Hyde Park in June. It was a Sunday.'

'You've thrown me. I was just being silly. You looked like Byron as a boy. So I thought, what about a poem, Byron?'

She seemed confused. I realised that this was a good thing.

'I actually got ten shillings once for a poem. In Trafalgar Square. From a Maltese woman. Her son had died in the war. She said I looked Maltese.'

'You could be. A Maltese Byron even. Well I'm blowed. I've met a real street poet.'

She did not take the hint about the ten shillings as I upped the 'ask' by at least 500%.

She took my hand.

'You look quite unclean boy.'

'I had a bath a few days ago in cold water in a house in Gloucestershire. But they had a party last night and I got drunk and dropped a girl in the fire.'

'This is getting more interesting. You dropped a girl in the fire?'

'She wanted me to take her upstairs and well, do things to her. But I'd had a few ciders. And what with one thing and another, she also weighed a ton, I dropped her as we passed the fire. They threw me out. These students who'd asked me to stay. But the cunts changed their minds.'

'You use 'cunt' in a non physical sense.'

'Is that good or bad?'

'That is good. Girls don't like to think you are referring to their actual recesses.'

I laughed. I knew a recess was another word for a hole. I hate the word hole. Many boys in Fulham and Chelsea called girls' parts holes. A hole was a lifeless thing. I preferred recesses.

I could see I had caught her. Who knows, I might get a pound out of this meeting. Then I would sleep in my old school bike shed and then in the morning go and have breakfast at the Chelsea Dining Rooms. Or even go down to Westminster and go to the coffee stall opposite the Abbey. The centre of the earth was that place. Open morning noon and night.

'The money, Miss. You did promise.'

But she ignored what I said and proceeded as if I had said nothing.

'You'll need a bath before we actually join the party.'

'Party, Miss? I just want ten bob, Miss. If you've got it. You look the class of person who might have ten bob to give to a boy whose been driven out of home.'

She laughed.

'Look! There's me making assumptions about you and you about me. The party is there. Yes?'

She pointed towards a door of a house opposite the bookshop. I looked at the middle class door. Who ever lived the other side of that door had money, I reasoned. Perhaps I could get to stay the night. A bike shed is preferable to a doorway. A couch in a front room is preferable to a bike shed.

'Yes, Miss, I would very much like. Do I get ten shillings? And do I get to eat? Anything. I'm so hungry I'll eat shit if it's camouflaged.'

She laughed.

'A boy with words! You won't have to eat shit boy. Only good food, brought up from the country. Made by honest hands.'

'Any tea? I don't drink coffee.'

'Tea. With sugar. Even a beer.'

'I don't drink, Miss. Except loads of cider.'

'No cider, boy.'

She took my hand and led me across the street from John Sandoes. I had been planning on climbing the wall of my old school – St Thomas Moore's Roman Catholic Secondary Modern School. And sleep in the bike shed at the bottom of the playground. It was a Friday night so there would be no school in the morning. The last time I had climbed that wall it was to get into the school and go to the headmaster's office. And smash it up and write 'Cunt' in letters across his wall. But now I was a runaway, sleeping rough having jumped bail, and all the old 'hates' with teachers and head masters had paled. All I had to do was survive and not get arrested.

We mounted the steps to the top floor. As she went I saw her great middle class arse swing back and forth and had a desire to fondle it, bite it and poke it. Ever since I had seen my first naked middle class arse at Christmas the year before I was obsessed with the middle classes and the arses of the girls of the middle class. We reached the top floor and she opened the door and walked into a warm, well decorated flat with three girls sitting on sofas. The room seemed full of sofas. Any one of them would have been preferable to St Thomas Moore's bike shed. I looked and in wonder almost collapsed into a sofa. But before I could do it my rescuer had to introduce me.

'Girls, look what I have got. My own little down and out. And he's a genuine street poet.'

The three girls, one brunette, the others golden-haired like my rescuer, screeched a strange-sounding welcome. I nodded 'hello'.

'Looks very 'Oliver' like.'

'Oh he's not. He's genuine.'

One came up close and smelt me.

'Bit rank.'

Causing them to giggle in unison. My hostess took me into the bathroom and ran the bath. She did not ask me. And undressed me. I stood stupefied. She took off my big RAF coat that Mick the Mouth and Brain had given me when I stayed on their floor in the World's End. It was their father's, who was a porter in the Science museum at South Kensington, a leftover from the war that he would not need. Not unless they reran the Second World War and we lost this time.

She took off my jacket that I had found in a bag out the back of the Royal Court Theatre. It was Edwardian. I looked good in it, fitting well, except that it was a woman's and had a very narrow waist. My trousers were denims that I had had for about six months and now they were dirty and ragged in parts. The big surprise was when she took off my trousers and looked at my grim underpants.

'Ugh! They need a good washing. In fact you and everything you are wearing needs a good dousing and cleaning.'

She pulled down my underpants and saw my erection.

'What a sight. I'd like to see that when you're a man. Now off with those poor socks.'

The socks were all torn and dirty. She said they would have to be thrown out. Then I climbed into the bath and she began washing me with a big sponge and shampooing my hair. Within minutes I was a cleansed and changed boy. She called in her friends and they all looked at me, one commenting that even though I was a boy I already had a good arse. Big towels came from a cupboard and I was rubbed by the group of them, causing me again to get an erection. My rescuer said what she had said before, that she was looking forward to what I looked like when a man and not a skinny undernourished boy. I took all of this in my stride. This was much better than St Thomas Moore's bike shed. And having been on the road, sleeping rough for over two months, ever since I jumped bail and ran away from home, I was looking for some comfort. The two days in a student cottage in the country was not too good as I had to sleep on the floor with one blanket. And they had not given me a towel to wash with. And the water was cold.

It was heaven with three middle class girls with fine arses and good tits.

We had the party. I was now in

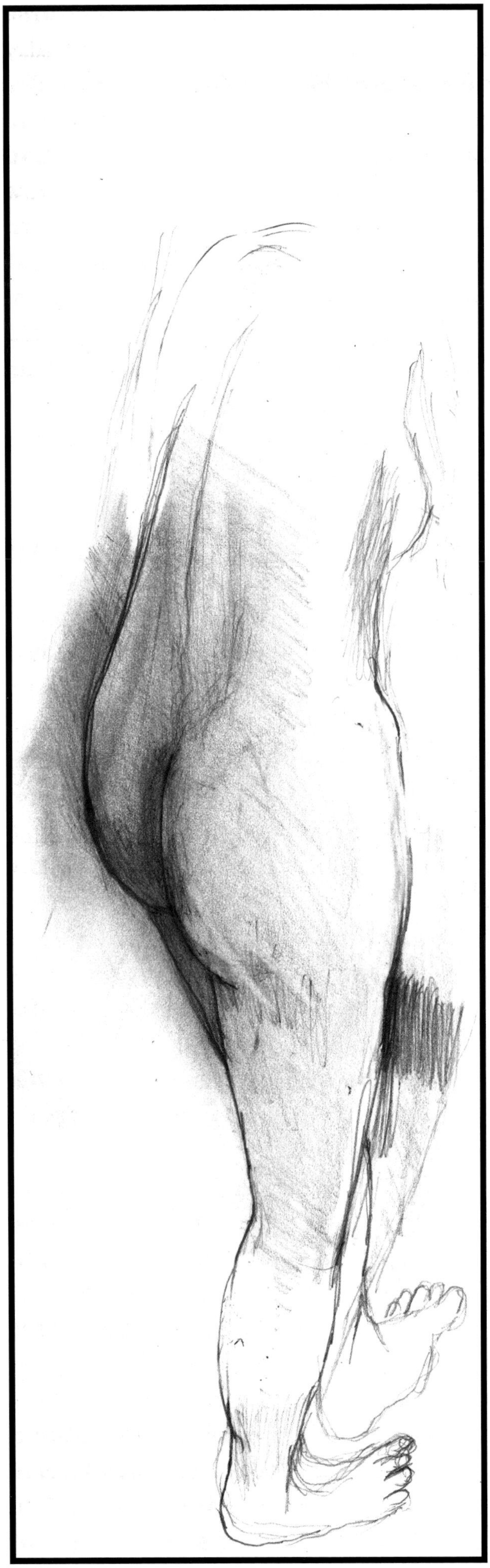

girls' clothing. I wore a green blouse that kind of looked like a shirt. I had clean underpants but in fact they were knickers. With wispy bits of lace and uncomfortable to wear. If I got arrested now they would laugh at me at Stamford House or Ashford Boys Prison. What fun they would have had with a boy with long hair and girls clothes on. I'd be laughed at as some queer and pushed and bullied by cunts paid to look after me.

The party involved me eating all the food they could give me, with a bottle of Coke. The girls drank from one bottle of Champagne and one bottle of wine. But they were soon drunk and stupid, with each girl doing something that surprised and pleased me. They danced the Can Can throwing their legs high, showing me their drawers and stocking tops. And then one girl, the brunette, to the music of Edith Piaf did a kind of strip, ending up showing me her beautiful, solid and good arse naked. I sat feeling as if paradise had arrived around the corner from my old school. When I saw her naked arse I felt like jumping on her and biting her. But I didn't. I did not know where a desire to bite arse came from. I was a good catholic, most times. But arse biting: it seemed a strange desire. I hoped that I would grow out of it even as I sat and looked and desired.

The girls drifted off back to their rooms. My rescuer, who was called Vanessa, took me into her room with mad eyes.

'How old are you boy?'

'I'm called Tony Bird.'

'How old are you Tony Bird?'

I always lied.

'Sixteen Miss. Last January the 30th I was sixteen.'

She looked at me with a kind of nice, friendly drunk face. I had to laugh.

'Why are you laughing boy? Sorry, Tony.'

'Because I am so happy. This is like heaven for me Miss. Sleeping rough for two months. Except for two days with some students. Who were cunts to me.'

She laughed.

'You do have a way with the word 'cunt'. It is poetical. It seems different when you say it. As if it is natural.'

'How old are you, Miss?'

'I'm very old. I'm eighteen. And you can call me 'V'.'

'That's a good letter. 'V' for Vagina.'

We both laughed. Then she got serious.

'I have a task for you, boy. Sorry, Tony. Have you ever tied anyone up before?'

'Only my mate's sister. She liked it. Down by the river in Putney. But we were about twelve then.'

'Then you must tie me up.'

She jumped off her bed. The room was clean and full of soft things. Pink seemed to be everywhere. She gave me a short piece of rope.

'Tie my hands behind my back, Tony, please.'

I did as I was asked. The girl by the river when I was twelve wanted to be tied up to show that she could escape. Which she did, even though we tied her very tight. She was very good at wriggling. V had some other plans that I could not get. I tied her and she lay on her bed with her back to me.

'There's a cane there, Tony. Take the cane and beat my bottom.'

This was getting difficult. Of course later I would understand. Especially after seeing Maggie Gyllenhaal in *The Secretary* which I saw when I was in California. But back then no one had prepared me for this perversion. I knew of other perversions, like men with boys. But I had not known then that there was this kind of strangeness. I also knew there were men who did things to dead bodies. But spanking women's arses was new to me.

'Miss. I got thrown out of school for not taking the cane. I hate the cane. How can I hit you with the stick?'

The cane was just like the one that got me barred from school for the last six months of school life. The headmaster had said he wanted me to not go to school and they would still fill in the register. All because I had taken the cane off of a teacher and threw it wildly into a corner. And then said, 'Fuck you. No one's fucking hitting me again, you cunt.' This was to the teacher whose job it was to administer the punishment. This time for hitting some arsehole in the corridor who had jumped the queue for school dinners.

'Take the stick, boy. And give me some gentle spanks on the bott. Please, Tony.'

I did the spanking with the stick, but she kept saying it was too soft. So I did it harder and harder. And then lifted up her skirt and she started to moan. I carried on looking at her arse and the marks I was making. I loved the look of her rear, with her lacy knickers and suspenders and stockings. I had suffered since I was twelve wanting to look up girls' skirts. And here I was, but doing something that felt wrong and perverse.

Icouldnotpreventmyselffrompulling down her knickers and carrying on. And soon she was red all over, her big, strong middle class arse. I untied her and she kissed me with her tongue going down my throat. But when I asked her to take my cock in her mouth or pussy she refused. We fell asleep. I was broken from all the roughing it. I needed nothing more than sleep. Even though this was a weird thing to do and a strange way to spend a Friday night and Saturday morning I felt good in V's bed. Clean and full of her snores. I just slept.

I woke in the morning and all I could remember was that I had been picked up. I woke to find myself naked, with the covers pulled back. I was sticky.

I had had a dream. But standing over me with a sketchpad was V. She was drawing me.

'Still, boy. Don't move.'

'Cut the fucking boy.'

'Sorry, Tony Bird. I'm drawing you.'

I lay still. I was hungry. Then she stopped and showed me the drawing. It was kind of good. But I thought I could do as good.

'Lay down. I shall draw you.'

'I've got to go and get some bread.'

'Please.'

She pulled off her gown and lay, in the same position that I lay in. I started to draw my first truly naked girl. I had seen parts of girls. But I had never seen a completely naked girl. I could not stop myself and whenever she asked if she could go and get some bread I pleaded with her to stay. After an hour I had done a very reasonable drawing.

'I go to Chelsea School of Art. It's down the Kings Road.'

'I know it. I used to pass it when I went to school. This drawing stuff is good stuff.'

'You may well have a talent, Tony Bird. Now I must get some bread.'

As she walked away I saw her soft and strong arse. And I saw the marks that I had left upon them. I felt I had disfigured her. Would her arse return to its former purity?

Surrey Countryside. 1962.

We marched across the cut grass towards a bridge. At the bridge we were told to stand easy. Some boys who knew how to run bounced up and down as if they knew they were impressive and were going to win. I stood and watched the seasoned ones. I could not run. I could sprint. I could scamper over roofs and climb up drain pipes. But I could not run steadily, scientifically, for three miles across country, towards some distant culvert, and then turn and run back. I had already failed the three-mile run the week before and had fallen on the roadside, breathless. But now they had ignored my entreaties to be allowed to sit the six-mile run out. That it might kill me. That I was only skin and bone. That I probably had asthma. That, that, that; but he did not listen, the master of this race, one of the people who ran our institutional lives from 15 until 20 years of age. And could do what they wanted with us.

'You, you filthy piece of shit, boy.'

'Yes, sir, that's me.'

'Dirty tike who can't take his medicine and runs away. Try running away today. And I'll make sure you spend the rest of your sentence locked up in Strangeways.'

He didn't like me. A few weeks before I had run away on his watch. And got to London. And with a mate had smashed up a car. Now back I was, being made to suffer. And anything I couldn't do he got joy out of making me do. Hosanna, you could see it writ on his mean, pigged, screw's face.

'Off, tike!'

I was directed to run off ahead of the other 'honoured' boys. Honoured because they accepted their sentences. And did not try to run. Did not try to escape from the dumb regime they imposed on boys who had done wrong. The screw who hated me seemed to love the boys who kowtowed to the rules.

The screw stood in his singlet and shorts, his plimsolls, bouncing like a man waiting to prove how good he was. His breath throwing out fiery hotness. He was strong and he could outrun anyone. His big arms and thick body obviously the result of all the hand to hand combat he did against Nazis in the war. Probably a dab hand at cutting throats with a bayonet, or with a quick twist of the neck giving an instant death.

I puffed and wheezed my way across grasses and through bushes. I looked left and right to see if there was a road I might take. I could trick my way on to a bus or a train. Or hitch a lift. I was already a seasoned con man. I knew how to talk people into doing things for me. But as I ran I knew that even I could not have got to London without any clothes except a singlet, and a pair of bland blue shorts. And black plimsolls that had 'BIRD' written on in white paint by the sewing room, who gave us all our clothing. Even I in winter would have thought this too foolhardy.

Boys now passed me exhilarated at their own speed. I coughed and wheezed and carried on aware that I would have to do this until I learned how to do it. As I went I could not but notice all the birds that got out of the way. Or shrilled and sung. The rich greens of the grasses even in winter. And the fine silver birches that, thin and tall, leant and stood. I tried to think of this nature and not of the run. Not of my young untrained lungs. My urban lungs that were only used to spurts of action to get away from a foe.

More boys passed and, uniformly, called me 'a prized cunt'. I would have called them prized cunts if I got the chance. The fact that they were and I was not was beside the point. They knew how to run and accept the abjectness of their sentences. And would be good and get out soon, cowards before the system.

We got to open fields where the farmer had ploughed up to clods, making it difficult to run through. Now my plimsolls got clogged with earth and my feet were wet and my lungs were about to blow. I wheezed and wheezed and spat, dribbled my life away. A rise in the ground threatened my chance of carrying on. I would not make the top of the small Surrey hill that had a mixture of big and small trees. I would have to lay down and the screw could then come and kick me and rubbish me. And tell everyone I was one who could run away but could not take my medicine and run.

By the hill I knew it was all over. At the brow of the hill my lungs seemed to go into a strange contraction, followed by an involuntary expansion. My mouth opened and my legs seemed to lose their weakness. And then I was over the brow of the hill and a violent opening and closing of my lungs turned to a rhythm.

And then it was as if I had been gifted new lungs. The slow, the old, the weak, the wheeze seemed to go and I was running on new legs and with new breath. I started to pass boys who had just passed me. My legs worked independent of me. They raced and ran ahead, passing even more boys. Unable to believe it, I thought I might be kidnapped by some spirit that had invaded my body. I was being spirited away to some other place. Maybe at last Jesus Christ had listened to my pleas to be taken from this Protestant world, full of non-believers with their grey churches. And I would meet Jesus at some rainbow foot.

As I ran I noticed not just the boys I passed but even more of the silver birch. And the great big oaks. And I decided that when I got back to the big house, after showering and supper, I would take some paper and pencils and draw what I saw on my run.

Ahead of me was a great horse chestnut and I tried to memorise its big outline, with its bare branches. I would draw it. I would draw it as it was to me as I ran by it.

The boys fell back and I went on. Now I could run further and further. Some boys dropped, or stopped for a rest. I carried on. The screw soon caught up with us and passed almost everyone, even though he was the last to start. And then he came level with me. He looked at me slightly ahead of me. I put on more speed and passed him. He then pulled past me. We did this again and again until we got to culvert where we were to turn and run back. He could not fuck with me. I would fuck with him. I would show that I was the strong and he was

only the weak. Along with all the weak 'prized cunts' he championed.

Now I did not notice the trees, nor the grasses and the birds that bounced out of our way. I kept running as fast and steady as I could and it seemed too soon to be back at the bridge where only a few boys had got to. They sat or leant forward. I did not stop. I ran on over the bridge across the big grasses in front of the house. I ran on, passed the fallen oak tree that fell one stormy day. I kept running and down the side to the lower corridor and even ran its length to the showers. I was the first. I stripped off, took my towel and went over to a shower and let the cold become hot. Then I stood and showered and rubbed soap into me. I stayed there for half an hour, until boys came in, some shouting at me that the running screw had sent out the word that I had run off. And that the police would have been notified. But I kept showering, enjoying the hot water more than I ever had. I only got out when he came in and stood in all his dirt looking at us, looking at me. He said nothing. I did not offer some excuse. I got out and got dressed and went to my house room to wait for my supper. Afterwards I would begin the drawing of the tree that was on the hill that I passed.

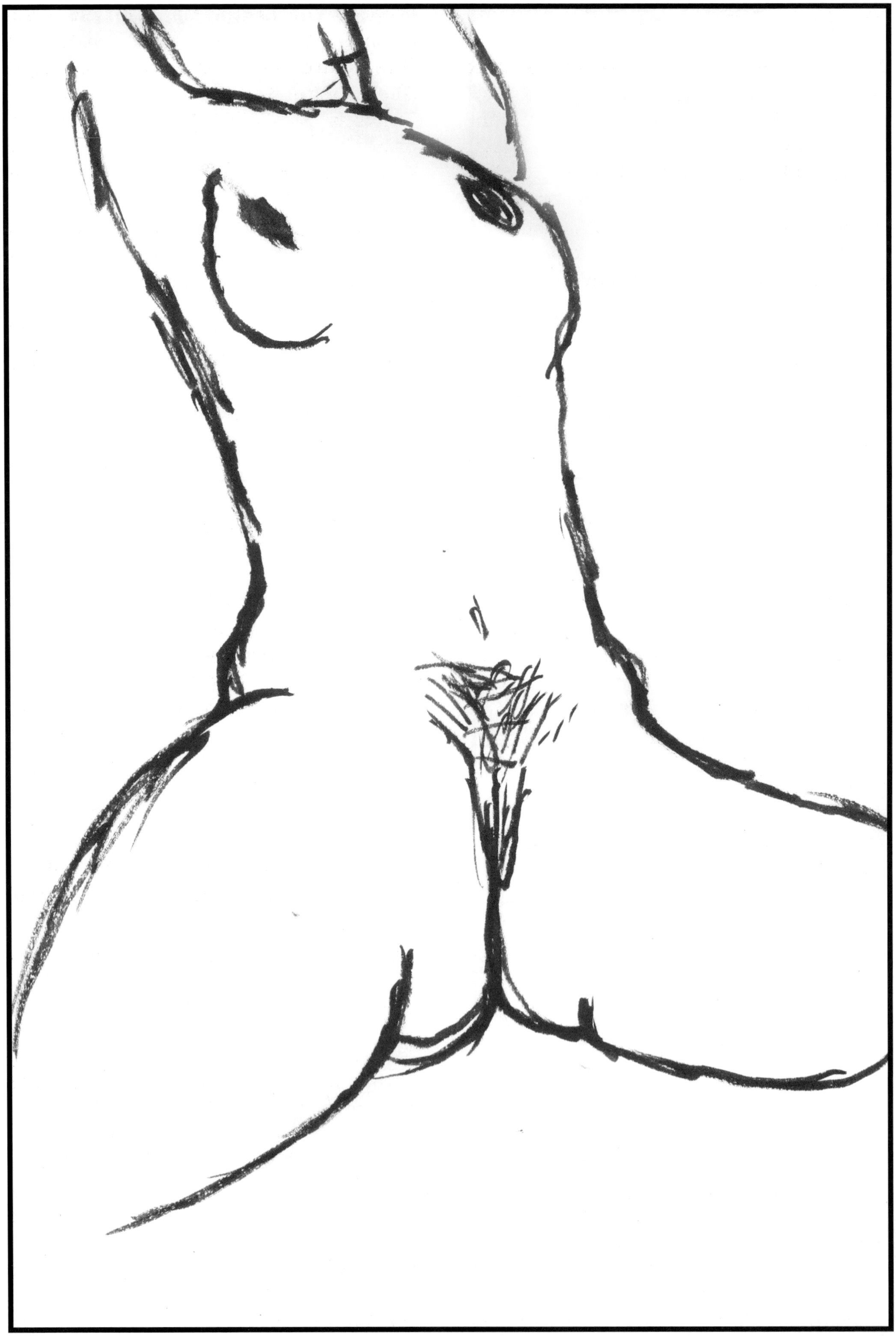

British Museum. 1964.

I was at the British Museum and it was a wet Sunday afternoon. I had my sketchpad and half a dozen pencils rammed into a top pocket. All good and sharp, from HB to B5. My pencil sharpener was in my pocket, along with a gum rubber. I also had water colours and a water bottle and a small palette in another pocket. I was loaded down and happy and sketching stuff in the Japanese rooms of the museum.

I walked to a small gallery and a girl was sitting on the floor. I stepped over her. She had no modesty, showing her stocking tops and the white tops of her legs. She smiled as I walked past with my drawing book. I went a few rooms along but was drawn back to the girl. I returned and stood above her. She looked up.

'Are you drawing?'

I said yes and squatted down beside her and looked at what she was drawing. She was drawing a mask from Japan and it was well drawn. Better than I could do.

'You're good.'

She smiled and asked if she could look at my book. We sat and we looked at each other's books.

'I want to be a painter.'

'So do I. Do you go to art school?'

'No. I go to art classes in secondary schools. I work for the Royal Borough of Kensington in their gardening department.'

'How old are you?'

I was back to telling the truth.

'18 at the end of this month.'

'I go to Chelsea art school.'

'I know it. I live near there.'

'You should come to the evening classes at Chelsea. For life drawing. No one asks.'

The museum closed and she asked me to have a tea with her opposite the museum. I fell in with her and we crossed the street. In the café I sat looking at this dark-haired girl, with fine white skin, and very red lips. She spoke to me as if I was a serious person. 'I like the way you draw. It's kind of innocent. As if you were not looking at it with some control.'

'Really? I look at watercolours by Constable. And at Girtin and Cozens. But I love John Sell Cotman best.'

'What do you think of Turner?'

'I think he's a cunt.'

Shealmostspitoutthehottea,gulping it wrongly.

'You feel that strongly?'

'I do. I think that way about Turner.'

She sat back and looked at me as if for the first time.

'I never heard anyone call a famous painter like Turner a cunt before. Who else is a cunt in the art world?'

'Reynolds? He's the only other cunt I can think of at the moment. Maybe Picasso is a cunt as well.'

She looked with a frown.

'I don't know how far you'll get in art if you look upon people as cunts.'

'Then maybe that's going to change. Maybe I am going to help change it.'

She looked even more perplexed.

'Have you had a hard life?'

'I don't know. It hasn't felt hard.'

'I mean rough? What kind of school and all.'

I thought about that question.

'Iwenttoacatholicsecondarymodern school. It was just ordinary. Then I was in trouble with the police. And got put away.'

Now she cheered up. She looked with renewed interest at me. So I told her more and more and she wanted to know even more. About rough sleeping, about prison and thieving. And being born in a slum. And she loved it. She sat so attentive that I told her all I could remember and even exaggerated it for her. And she lapped it up as I told her more and more, most true but some of it exaggerated.

The café closed and we sat looking at each other.

'Have you drawn a naked woman before?'

'I've drawn one. When I was 15. She was an art student who went to Chelsea School of Art.'

'But nothing since?'

The door closed behind us. We walked down and got the 14 bus. We would change onto the 22 at Hyde Park Corner.

'I drew a girl with red hair. But only her tits. It was the night that President Kennedy got shot. I didn't feel too good about continuing.'

We sat in the upstairs of the 14 bus and she looked hard at me.

'You speak very loudly.'

'That's because I've got a loud voice.'

She whispered almost.

'But you said 'Tits' with such great emphasis I think they must have heard you downstairs.'

'That's the voice I have. It was only tits as President Kennedy died. No fanny.

I felt so bad. The greatest catholic in the world.'

She spoke softly.

'We should remember we are not alone.'

'And as for that cunt Turner.'

I said this to just make an impression. She screwed up her face and said, 'Keep quiet.'

We got to Hyde Park Corner and got off to wait for the 22 that would take us down the Kings Road. She lived off the Kings Road, and I lived where it crossed into Fulham and became the New Kings Road. We talked at the bus stop.

'I think you referred to Turner in the bus to annoy people.'

'I did. I was having fun.'

'Are there a lot of 'cunts' in your life? I mean people who you call that name?'

'My mum and dad and brothers use it a lot. And blokes at work. I'm surrounded by the 'cunt' word. I suppose that makes me working class.'

'I suppose it does.'

The 22 arrived and we got on and sat close to each other. She looked at me carefully. I liked being looked at carefully, as if she was trying to work me out. We swung past the butchers shop at Knightsbridge that I used to work in, delivering meat to posh houses when I was 14.

'I worked there. That's where I saw my first naked girl.'

'You're obsessed with nudity.'

'I am. Of girls.'

'Tell me how you saw a naked girl in a butchers shop.'

I had to laugh.

'It wasn't in the butchers shop. It was when I was delivering.'

'You sound like a doctor.'

I had to laugh again. I laughed so loud that people looked over at me. If I was without the girl I would have told them to mind their own fucking business: looking at me as if I was a wrongdoer.

'Meat I was delivering.'

'Tell me about this meat.'

'I can't tell you about the meat. Only that I delivered it. Lamb, pork, chickens, sausages, chipolatas. It was the Queen's butchers as well as a general butchers. One day at just before 7am, just before Christmas in 1960, I climbed the stairs of the tradesmen's entrance all the way to the top floor.'

'You're still talking very loud.'

I whispered, loudly.

'I knocked on the door and a girl a few years older than me opened it. She had thick blonde hair, and only a thin nightie on. I could see everything. Everything, even the wispy little hairs round her 'Granny Grunt'.'

'Granny Grunt? What's that?'

'Granny Grunt, rhymes with Cunt.'

She looked around again, alarmed as my whisper was very loud.

'You get that word in everywhere.'

'It may be because I was brought up on it.'

'Continue with the story.'

So I carried on.

'I'd seen snatches of girls' bits. Bit here and bit there. But this was the first time I saw the complete thing, from tit to arse. Because as she turned round I saw the finest arse I had ever seen.'

We got to Sloane Square. I pointed out the street that led to St Thomas Moore's School, where I went as a boy. And then when the bus turned and went down the Kings Road I pointed out where I had been picked up and drawn by a girl who went to Chelsea School of Art, three years before. I pointed out John Sandoes bookshop where the girl had met me.

'What was her name?'

'Vanessa. Something.'

She did not know a Vanessa at Chelsea School of Art. Soon we passed the town hall and she got up.

'I live near here. Would you like to come back to my place?'

I looked at her great thick black curly hair. And her bright lips which every now and then she used lipstick on. And her white skin. Like a famous film star from the 1940s. English with great tits and a very strong and good arse. Like Margaret Lockwood, one of the most beautiful actresses in the world.

'That sounds like a good idea.'

'Maybe we can draw.'

We got off the bus stop not far from the art school and the fire station. We walked down Oakley Street. I pointed at the place where I slept in the back of a Ford Popular motor car for a month, on and off, with my big coat pulled up over me. It was the best place I had ever slept. I never felt safer than when as a rough sleeper I slept in the back of a motor car.

It was opposite where she had a room. We walked in and her room was on the ground floor. It was small, with just enough room for a bed and a table and a chair.

'It's more like a cell.'

'You should know.'

'But –.'

'But what?'

'But it's great. It's just enough. You would never need more than this. And it's tidy and clean. And the bed looks clean and sleepable in.'

'It is. Can I make you a cup of coffee? There's a kitchen out the back.'

I went out with her to the kitchen. I didn't want to stay in the room in case she might think I would steal something. And then if something went missing she would blame me. You had to watch with middle class people. They could blame you if you weren't clever.

We went back to her room and she sat on the bed and I sat on a chair. She smiled at me.

'I feel so relaxed with you. Even though I've heard more 'cunts' today than I have ever had in the whole of my life.'

'I think there'll be more around. When *Lady Chatterley's Lover* was published, 'Cunt' was let loose. Once the middle classes use the word it'll be in books and everywhere. There may even be new shops. Like 'Cunts Corner'. I bet you. You'll walk down the Kings Road in ten years time and there'll be 'Cunts Corner'. And 'The Cunt and Flower', and pubs with names like that.'

She looked at me and did not smile. I may have been funny. But it might have been wearing thin. Or she was thinking of something.

'How old are you?'

'20.'

'Where are you from?'

'Sudbury. Where Gainsborough comes from.'

'I fucking love Gainsborough's drawings and water colours. And paintings of nature. *Cornards Wood* is my favourite.'

'Would you like to draw me?'

'I would draw you at the drop of a hat.'

'Have you got a hat?'

'At the drop of a pencil.'

'I feel like being drawn. I have this overwhelming desire to be drawn. By you.'

I sat and watched as she sat up and undid her blouse, as her black bra came into sight. She undid the bra and there they were. Two strong tits before me. Then she pulled off her very short skirt. And stood up and there were her black knickers that I had seen at the beginning. She undid her stockings and then took off her knickers. Her black pubic hair was bushy. I had never seen anything like this before. Then she took off her suspenders. I wished she would have left them on. She lay on the bed.

'The Naked Maja.'

'Wow.'

I commenced. Soon I was lost in the drawing. We did not speak. She looked hard at me, but I just carried on drawing. I drew for over an hour and was tired with the concentration.

'Tomorrow night you must come to the art school at six. I will meet you outside and we will walk in together. Then we will draw. No one will say a word to you. But you can't look gauche. You have to look as if you fit in.'

I watched her dress. When she got to her suspenders I moved onto the bed and kissed her. And touched her. And she kissed me and allowed me to play with her. She smiled and said nice things. But it wasn't going anywhere.

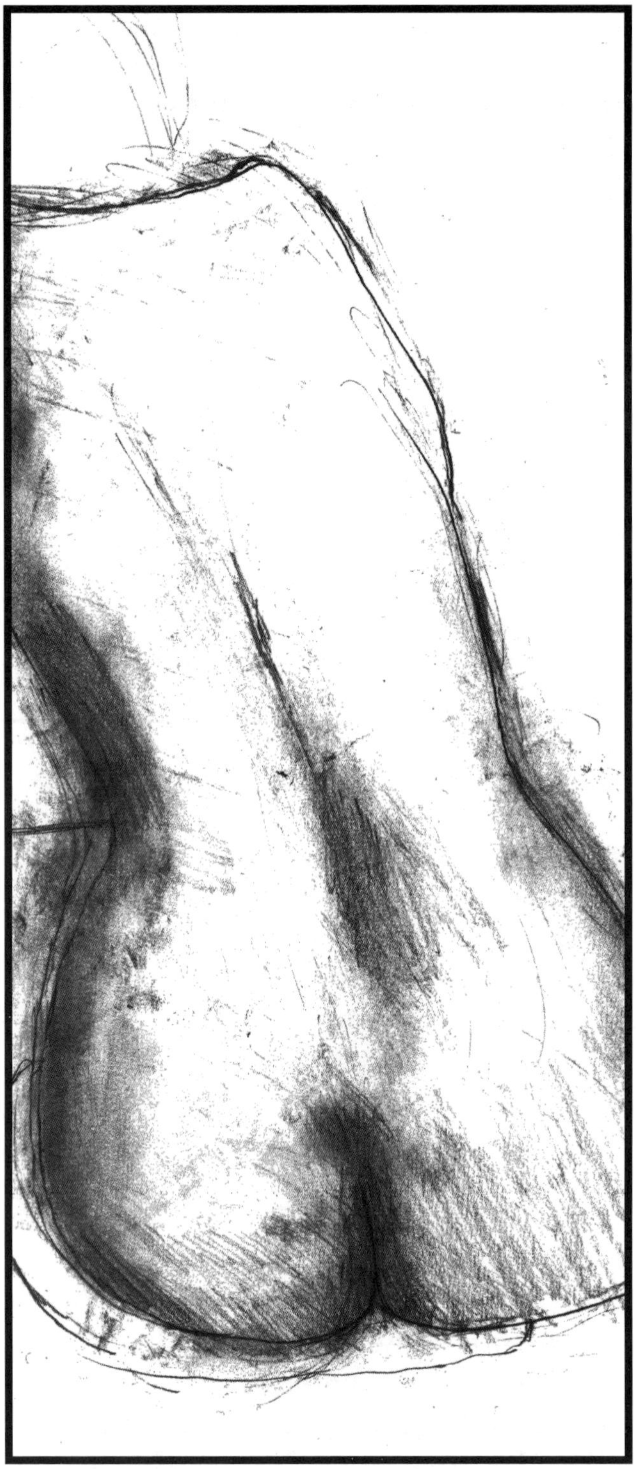

'You are an odd ball to be into art.'

I met her the next night. I spent the whole day frightened that I might have played her wrongly. Would she be there? Had I played the working class goat too much? Did I have to use the 'cunt' word so often? Surely I should know polite society doesn't like cunts and stuff.

But she was there. She stood by the steps of the school near the old library. A place I had passed throughout much of my childhood. On the way to school, or to shop lift along the Kings Road. On the corner I had begged on occasions from middle class people, telling the story of my dying mother, and her last moments in an iron lung. I had fought with boys on the Kings Road, and on building sites. And now I was going into an art school.

'Are you nervous?'

'I'm shitting myself.'

'I thought you might have a dramatic answer.'

We walked along the corridor to the far room, which was big and full of students already working at their easels. There were two models, one a thin looking man, and the other an old looking woman. But I got to an easel and began. And kept drawing, and drawing, ignoring what was going on around me. At the break I noticed that my friend had gone. I was on my own. That suited me. My fear had gone.

I went every night. Straight from work, getting there at six. The 49 bus from Kensington High Street was a godsend, allowing me to make the journey in half an hour. And then I would draw and draw, and gain in strength. Often the models were not great beauties. But it did not matter. Big women seemed easier to draw. The bigger the woman, the easier to capture her quickly. I became friendly with the masters who taught us, or suggested improvements.

And then one night, a few months after I had started, I called the master aside. He was a fine French man who talked very carefully and sincerely to me.

'Sir, do you think I should apply for art school.'

He looked at me with some concern.

'I thought you were already at art school?'

'No. I just come to the classes.'

He became very animated.

'Then you must apply. Go to the office tomorrow and get on the list. They are choosing just now.'

It was March. The next day I went to the art school office and spoke to a man.

'I would like to apply for the art school for next year, sir.'

'Oh, sorry, but we have got our list of candidates.'

My face must have done something to him. He took a pencil and wrote my name at the end of a typed list. And told me that I would have to be at The Regent Street Poly on the following Friday at 2pm. With my portfolio.

I rushed back to work and cleared and cleaned the little garden I was in charge of. And then at home that night chose loads of drawings that I had drawn and painted over the previous two years, while in reformatory. I made up my folder and went to bed excited. I had a great chance of getting into college. I told myself I was very good.

The Friday came and I did not have good clothes to wear. The only decent pants I had were too short, so I looked like a hillbilly. I had no jacket and came in a shirt only. And I had a large portfolio that was difficult to carry to the college at Oxford Circus.

When I got there I sat on a bench. There were girls with thin black portfolios. They talked among themselves. Where were the boys? Every now and then someone would take someone's portfolio and ten minutes later call them in. I was the last and waited the whole afternoon. At last I was the only one left. Someone came and took my portfolio and then went into a room. I waited ten minutes, then twenty, then half an hour. It occurred to me that they had forgotten about me, or rejected me because I was the last on the list. I got up and walked around, and had worked out already what to say to the 'cunt' who would come and tell me I had missed the boat.

After 40 minutes the door opened and a man led me into a big room. And on all the walls, covering the walls, was a drawing or painting by me. I was astonished. Two years of my work, with some of the new stuff. All out on the walls. And the committee who decided sitting looking at me as if I was someone very special. A vast exhibition of all that I had chosen to keep in my portfolio. A portfolio made of cardboard and painted, decorated all over.

The man who had added me to the list asked me questions. I answered as best I could.

'What do you do now?'

'I work for the Royal Borough of Kensington, in their parks and gardens and trees department.'

He turned and pointed to a plant on a window sill.

'What is that plant?'

'It's a pelargonium. A Zonal Pelargonium. Most people just call them geraniums.'

He was astonished. He asked most of the questions. Then he said, 'I think you will hear good news in the next few days.'

I left and waited outside while they took down the work and put it back in the portfolio. Then I left, and walked all the way to Hyde Park Corner, down the back streets and into Hyde Park. I was happy. I knew I was going on to the next stage.

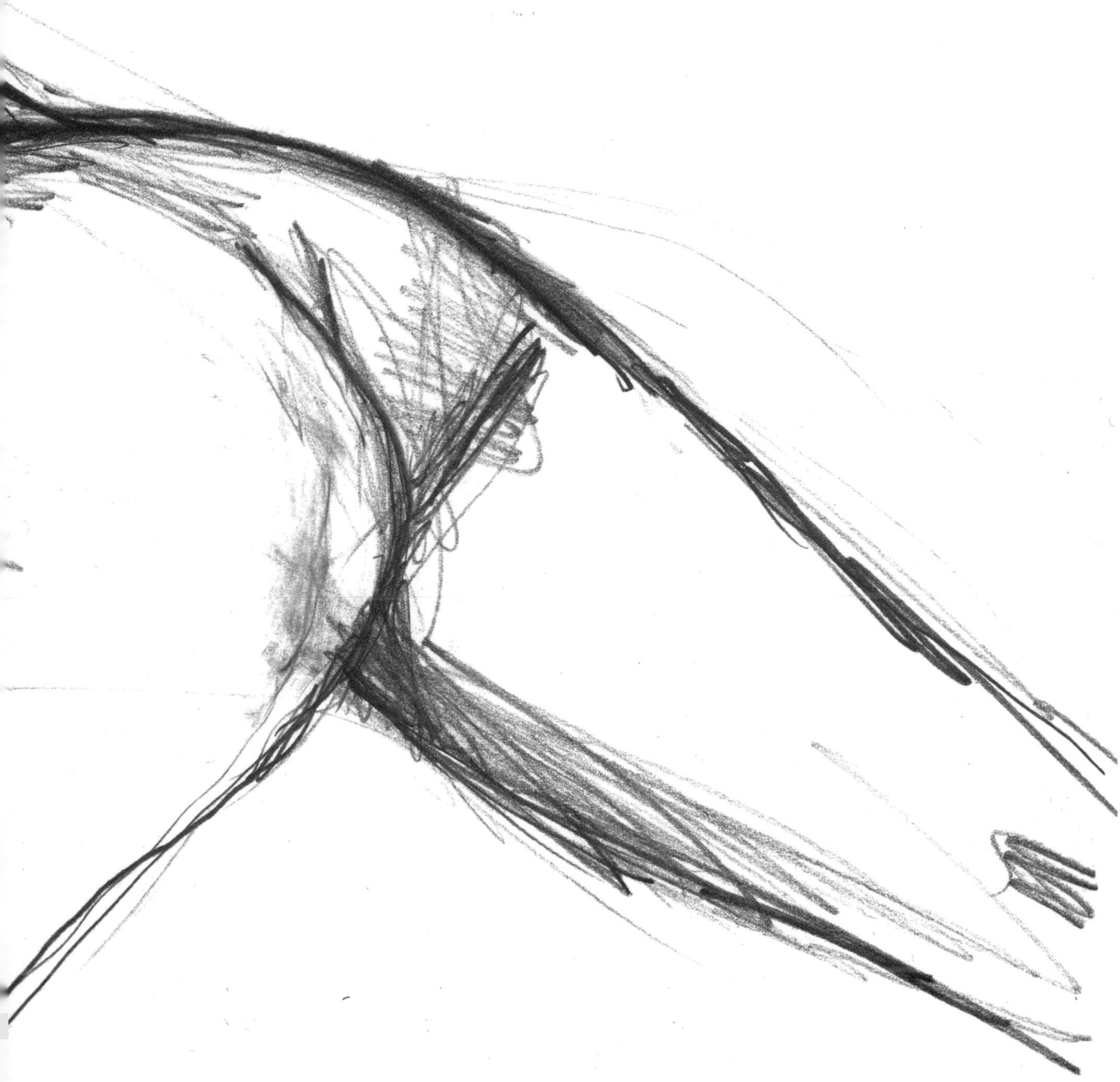

Kensington. 1964.

It didn't take long to get into the middle classes. Eighteen years. When I got in I realised they were not as bright as they pretended. They knew nothing about art. Nothing mattered deeply to them. It was all manners and eating. And making sure that they didn't embarrass themselves in public. I had a big breasted, well arsed, beautiful blonde middle class girl who ended it all because one night I vomited on her at her Christmas party. That was enough to break the spell.

A few months before the vomiting we walked around through the night holding hands, snogging, tit playing, cunt and cock rubbing. We got to St Thomas' Hospital on the south side of Westminster Bridge. Clara stood stupified as she looked over at the Houses of Parliament glowing in its winter lights.

'Oh, if I was a painter I would paint such a sight.' And she turned and looked at me with a kind of romantic look to her.

'You talk shit. Fucking shit. To think all the money your mum and dad spent on you and you've not got a cultural bone in your body. Your mind is just made up of shit thinking. One day you'll have matching wallpaper and paintings.'

'Well you, you barmy proletarian aren't exactly going to lead us into a promised land, are you? You can't even stop eating like a pig in a field.'

I grabbed her by the throat and bit her. She screamed in enjoyment.

'You vicious piece of shit. I want to marry you and keep you in a cave.'

'How do you explain the bites to your mum?'

'I tell her that it's Bonaparte. That's what we call you.'

'Bonaparte will do.'

We crossed Westminster Bridge. I had my hand up her dress and could feel her undercarriage. It made her excited that I had fingers in her just as we got to Big Ben. This was a different kind of London, she said. I was a different kind of world to her. She looked into my green eyes and at my black curly hair and said, 'You are my Bonaparte. You little bitter, tough, nasty invader. If you go into politics it will only be to murder people.' And the look on her face suggested that even if I did she would only get wet about it and not betray me. So long as I did not embarrass her in public, which the gallons of beer and Pimms Number One vomit did a good job of. I was ostracised. I could murder people for a political cause. But I could not throw up on their lovely pink Christmas dress.

Another night we went to a party at the newly opened London Hilton. We ended up in someone's room and Clara and I got behind the curtains and bit each other. She bit me hard and I bit her harder. And then I strangled her almost and she fell to the floor. She was sick. And then when she got up her eyes swum in deep love for me. A friend in a Mini drove us with a load of others to a park and we stripped off and jumped into the pool. I was as pissed as arseholes and licked a friend of her's cunt. This caused her consternation. When I tried to explain that it was just the drink she slammed the door on my face. I walked off down the Kings Road towards the Six Bells, determined to get rid of her. But she came to the Six Bells and bought me many drinks. And then took me to Picasso's for a Spaghetti Bolognese. And sat looking into my eyes.

'I fucking hate you Bonaparte. I fucking hate you You are a selfish user of people. But I would be lost without you. Please if you are going to lick someone's cunt in front of others, can it be me?'

'That is a promise I can easily make.'

She looked at me with great interest.

'The proles always have more fun than the posh.'

We walked home slowly. Though she was at school and I was at art school neither of us wanted to rush around for our studies. I walked her first, and then I walked off down to Brain's flat in the World's End. And got home about half past two. I could still taste Clara in the corner of my mouth.

The middle classes, the upper middle classes: they were people who money and houses and education was wasted on. It was better that they became the proletariat and us who were from underneath took a turn at the top. Then we could vaunt our ignorances.

At art school a girl with fine black hair stopped me in the corridor.

'You're a friend of Clara, aren't you?'

'I finger her, if that's what you mean.'

She looked perplexed.

'You what?'

'Finger her? I haven't got the cock in yet.'

She looked at me with great incredulity.

'You are obscene.'

'I think you'll find art schools are obscene. Lecturers shagging students. Both boys and girls. And late parties where dicks get sucked.'

'I'm only a first year.'

'I'm only a first year.'

'You've heard all about this?'

'I did. And I went to a party where the girls and the boys were sharing themselves around. Chelsea School of Arse, is what it should be called.'

'Did you share yourself out?'

'No. I am saving myself for Miss Right. Maybe you.'

She walked off. As she walked off I noticed that her arse was great in the pair of Levis she wore. But hers as of yet were too clean. Maybe when she had sucked a load of cocks at some art school party she might have dirtied up her Levis. And her mind.

I stood in the library looking around for the good-looking girls who were all in the older years. A very good-looking girl stood looking at a book on Matisse. I stood behind her and paused. She knew someone was behind her. She turned and looked at me. I smiled. She snarled.

'I love Matisse.'

She snarled even more. And put the book down.

'Well bully for you.'

And walked off. Her Levis were all torn and showed bits of knickers. And they were stained. As if things had dropped onto them. But her face and hair were clean. She looked back at me with a bitter smile. It was the smile of the cognoscenti looking at the novice. The older experienced looking back on the new intake. I smiled and waved and she looked pissed off. I would spend most of the term pursuing her. Even though she had a big boyfriend whom on occasions she threatened to call. To beat me up. I said, well if it

must be, it must be. I did see the big boyfriend around but he never said anything to me. And when I waved at her when he was there she snarled but did not tell him that an irritating first year was flirting with her every time I saw her.

You went into the big room and you stayed there for perhaps two and a half hours. And you drew. Then you had half an hour break. And then you went back for two hours. By which time your hand was sore from drawing. And your eyes seemed to see double. The concentration was intense.

Then in the afternoon you did more of the same. At five thirty you left. Or most left. I stayed on. I went to more drawing classes or print classes. I drew carefully and continuously. Working more and more at drawing. And out of this I hoped to prove nothing. I was doing what I wanted to do. What I had wanted to do since in the reformatory, having come back from a boys' prison, having run away, I decided I wanted to draw and paint. And from then on I had not deviated one step. I was going to draw and paint and do that until I died. There was nothing else on earth that could equal my commitment. That was the joy of the work. The total and completeness of drawing and painting. And being a serious person who did not just look at girls' arses. Or if you did it was to paint them or draw them. It was not a way of picking up girls. It was not a way to get some visual imagery going so that later you could wank in private over what you had seen.

Monastic: that is how it felt on those long days in Chelsea school of art. Drawing and painting pushed everything away. Until the last night of term and Clara's Christmas party. I had got drunk at lunch time. I had got drunk after school. And then I had gone to C's party and I drank all the Pimms Number One I could find. And soon the room was spinning and Clara was introducing me to someone. Her pink dress with her cleavage; and me suddenly, like a fountain throwing up all over her, probably filling her cleavage with puke.

That was the end of my friendship with Clara. She loved me. Loved my biting and my fondling. And almost fucking her. But at 17 she was still under the sway of her mother. One regurgitation and it was all over. We never spoke again. I was no longer her Napoleon, or Bonaparte. I was what I had always been: a despicable member of the underclass who puked in public on her.

I never got to do much drawing of Clara. One night when her mother was away I stripped her and spanked her. And then drew her. But the drawing was a variation of fondling. I drew her cunt and she loved the picture and kept it somewhere. She took it out of my sketchbook and when I noticed it had gone she said it was evidence and she wanted it. I did not argue. But out there somewhere is a drawing of a cunt: fulsome, half hairy, with the lips clearly delineated. Or maybe after the puking she tore it up and threw it away. Years later I saw her standing on the platform at Kensington High Street Underground station. I was on the other platform. I went and stood and looked over at her. She looked at me with a quizzical eye. My head was shaven. I had joined the revolutionary struggle. I was a factory worker, sent in by the movement to stir up the workers and try and create a situation politically conducive to revolutionary politics. I was not good at it. I had the sense that it was necessary for me to do. But I did not like doing it. It was like casting myself into a desert.

What a shocking world I was living in. That I had to give up drawing in order to save the world from barbarism. That I had to go back to the class that I came from and try and stir them to revolutionary action.

She looked over at me with a quizzical look. I was a man now, not a boy. Filled out, strong-looking. And without the mop of wild, made-in-the-18th-century hair. I waved at her and she half waved at me. Her train came and she got on it and looked from the window at me. It was a poignant moment for me. I was in exile. I was in exile in England, in London. But among the revolutionaries. And I had thrown art down to do revolution.

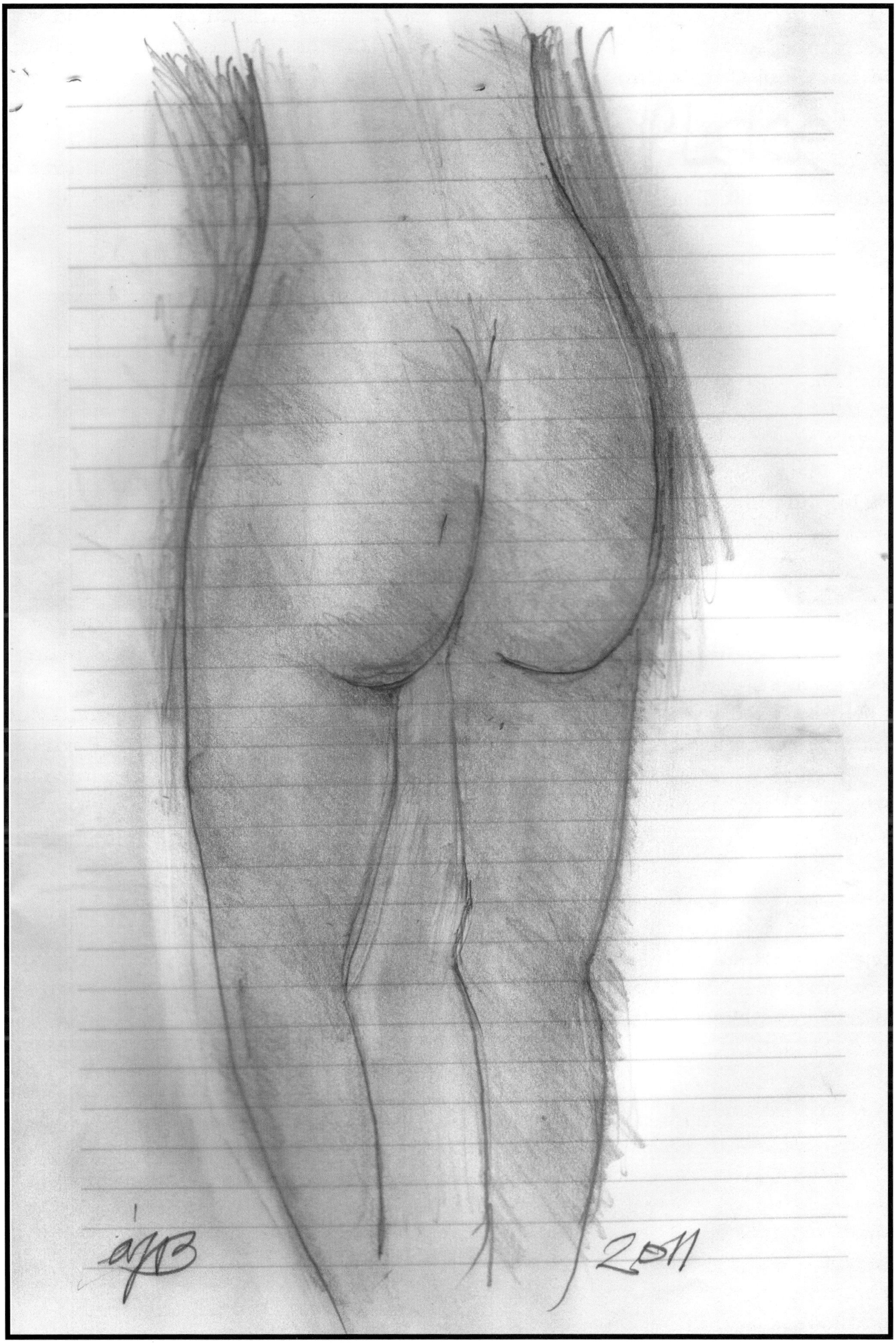
2011

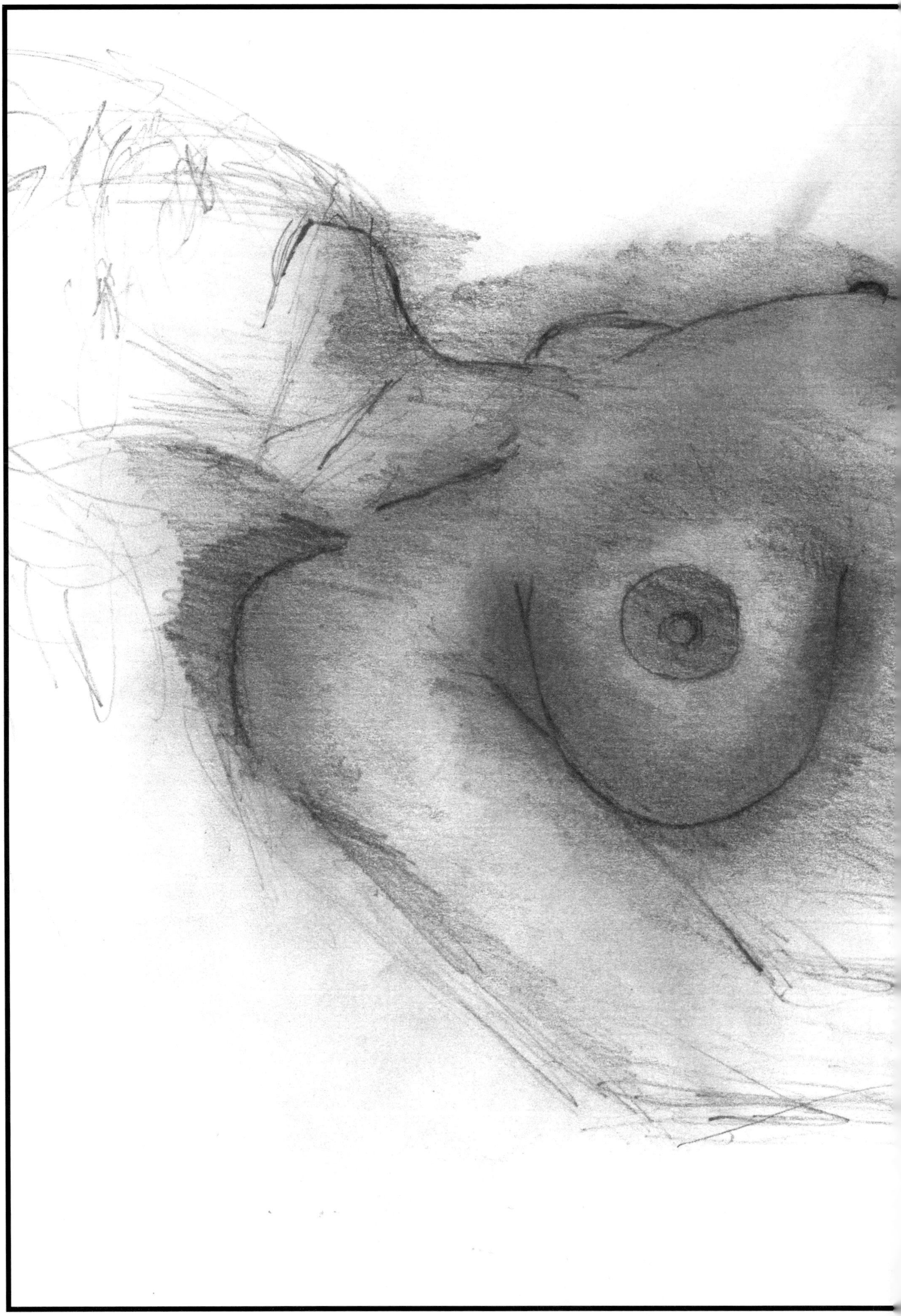

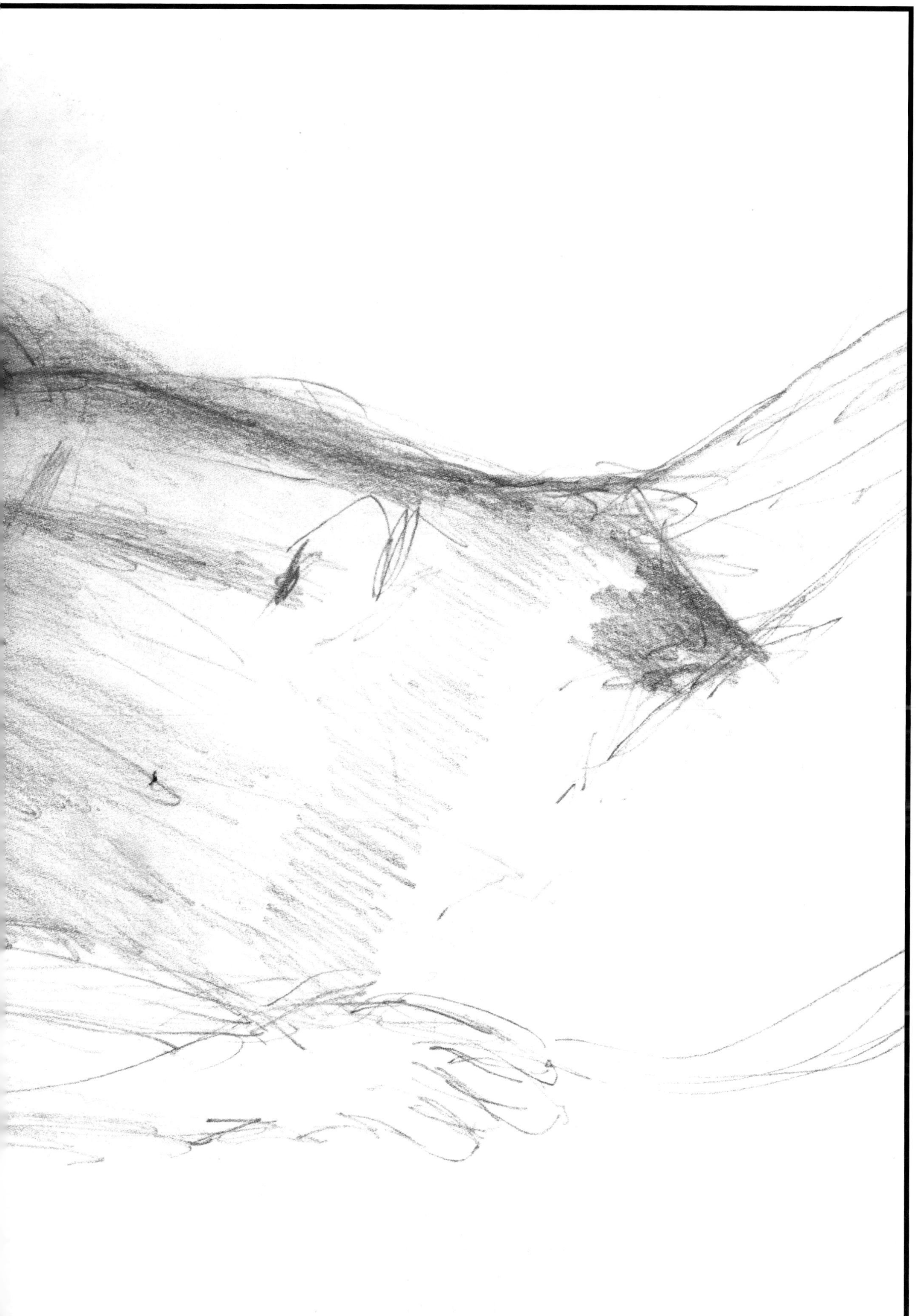

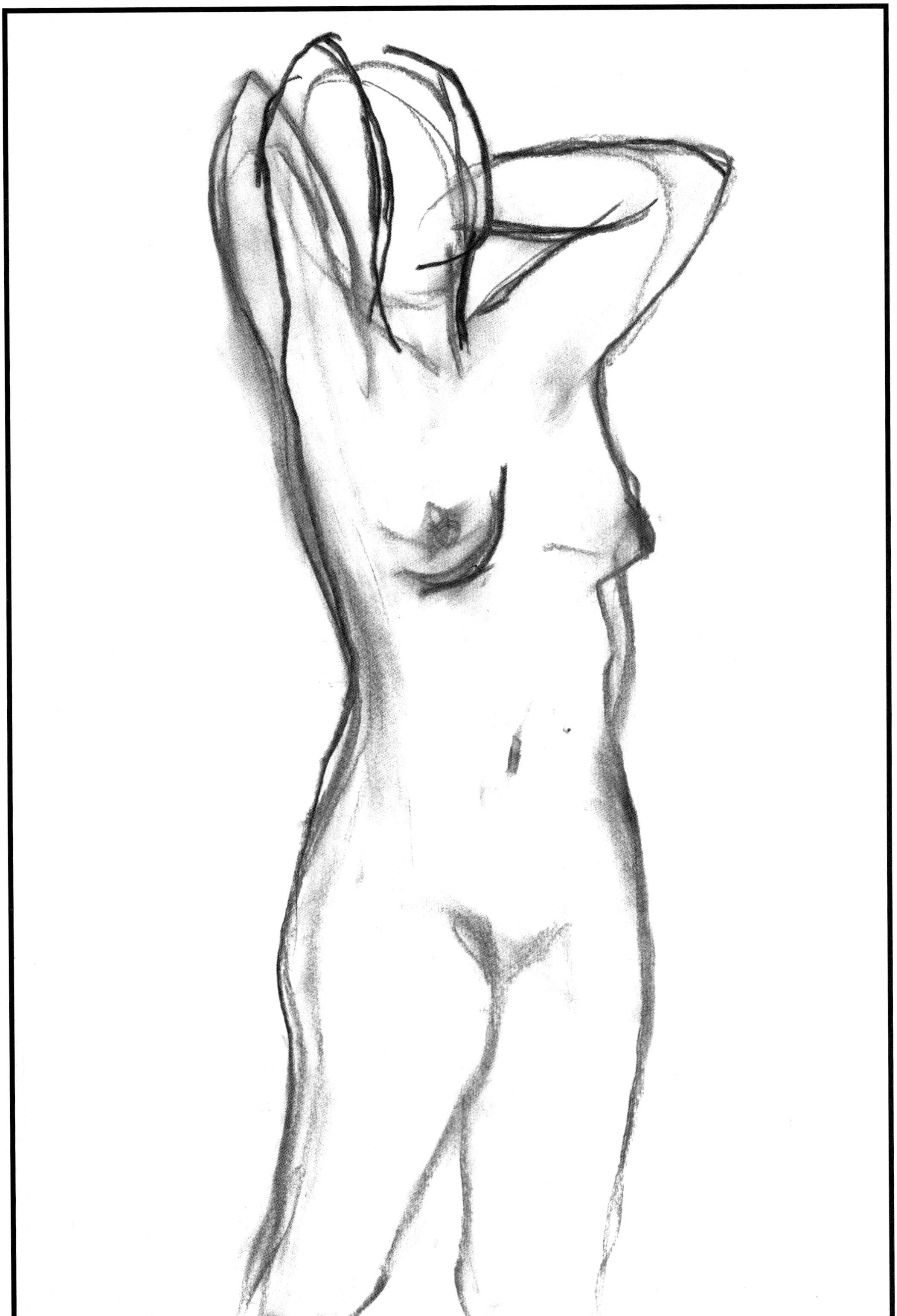

Soho. 1965.

London Night was to be joined with *Paris Night,* and eventually united with *New York* and then *LA Night.* Mr Tosservich – I am not sure about that spelling – asked me, was I good?

'You good boy?'

'I am capable of deep levels of hard work.'

He threw a hand about the air, just missing his nose.

'English people I don't understand even. So you wanna sell advertising for *London Night?* And this girl? She your lovebird?'

'We met on the stairs. Just now. She's come for a job as well.'

He laughed.

'I throw you two into bed too quickly. So Miss, you wanna sell for *London Night?*'

She snarled and turned up her nose.

'You are fucking disgusting. You fat Jew. Stick your job up your Jewish arse.'

He looked at me and smiled.

'Bad mouth. But pretty. You could do vorse. Me fat Armenian, not fat Jew, lady.'

She got up and walked to the door. At the door he called out loudly.

'Seven pounds ten shillings in your hand. And meals.'

She stopped. And turned. And changed the rake of her face.

'I like Jews normally. Fat or thin. When do we start? Can I get a sub? Say £3? Now.'

He put up his hands and threw them about.

'Come on. Name. Address. I give you money but you tell me how you sell.'

'Geraldine McGuire. 31 Tuppett Close London W2. Just off the Portobello Road.'

'So how you sell?'

'I use my tits. And my arse. Shall I show you?'

She sat on his desk and wriggled herself into different postures. I looked at her with increasing interest. Her 'Boat Race' was not all that interesting. But her arse and tits, and the way she moved, snake-like, was alluring. I imagined me drawing her. I could do the drawing and we could sell erotic drawings of her on the stalls of the Portobello Road.

'You sell like that? You're my man.'

He looked at me and screwed up his hardened face.

'How do you sell? She have something to sell. You? To queers only?'

'I sell you. Your magazine. Nothing has hit London, not in a hundred years. Explaining all of its attractions. Its beautiful restaurants. Greek, Turkish, Lebanese Indian, Italian. All races are represented in 1965 London. This magazine oozes good food and wine; and good sex.'

He looked at me.

'Ten shillings a week more for who sells more. Alright already?'

Geraldine McGuire stroked his face.

'Your magazine Mr Tosseroff: it's hot as buns, as warm as toast. Sex in pages. If it's me or him, tell him to fuck off Mr Tosseroff. Right now.'

She looked at me as she said this. When she leant forward her dress revealed her nipples. I had seen the dress in the window of Mary Quant on the Kings Road. Nipples that were flame red, as if she'd lipsticked them. I looked and could see that Geraldine

McGuire was not safe to be with.

'I take both. I need both. Last two cunts could not sell. But you be better boys, or I fuck you hard.'

He took out two five pound notes from a wad of notes. He gave the girl one five pound note and the other he gave to me.

'Tonight you come to Octopus. We go now. Knightsbridge. Crikey! Crikey, get cab.'

It was 5.30pm and I was supposed to meet Karen at Gloucester Road tube at 6pm, after her work. But now the sniff of money descended upon me. The wad of money turned us both. Crikey, his man, got in the cab with us. He was a bad smelling masturbator from Wimbledon who kept smiling and sweating and praising Mr Tosservich for his great ability to create new businesses out of the dust. As he praised Mr Tosservich sitting opposite us in the cab, he looked at Geraldine and her tits and smiled and sweated and talked about life in Wimbledon.

'Mr Tosservich escaped the Soviets young lady, young man. He got out and came to England and made money. Very quickly. Now *London Night* is going to change London. Night and day. Because Mr Tosservich has willed it so.'

Geraldine looked at me and with two fingers pretended she was shooting me. She screwed up her eyes. I wondered if I might not end up at 31 Tuppett Close, London W2 that night with narrow-eyed Geraldine sucking my membership. Or Geraldine at some penthouse sucking the dick of Mr Tosservich. With pounds in ten pound notes and loosely dropped fivers. Might I not share in her largesse?

By the time the traffic weathered Piccadilly and Knightsbridge and the back streets of Chelsea it was nearer six than ever. And I was nervous. Only a drink would obliterate the image of Karen, who would be waiting for me in the café at Gloucester Road. The club was a few dark rooms with some girls in. And a bar and a drink of whiskey was soon before me. I drank it quickly and had another. And then Geraldine became realer and the girl receded; and stayed receded all of that night.

Mr Tosservich and Geraldine disappeared down some back stairs and I was left with two big breasted girls and Mr Crikey. Mr Crikey smiled and sweated and as he told me about the honesty and genius of Mr Tosservich he stroked one of the big titted women's arse. He held up a tenner. A tenner was more than I had ever earned in a week. I looked at Mr Crikey and wondered: was there a weakness within him I could exploit? There was; it was sex. He joined everyone else in London in 1965 who thought only of sex.

As he stroked, he told me of the genius of Mr Tosservich and that I would learn a lot from him, young man.

'But will I earn a lot out of him, Mr Crikey?'

'It's Mr Crickley, young man. Mr Tosservich cannot quite get it.'

'You don't think he's taking the piss do you?'

Mr Crikey cleared his throat.

'Mr Tosservich does not 'take the piss', young man. He is a serious businessman of great obduracy and good fortune. A true gentleman.'

'But probably being sucked stupid

by his new recruit.'

Mr Crikey stopped playing with the woman's buttocks and breasts. He still held the tenner in his hand. He put it back in his wallet, where other notes were in evidence.

'Mr Tosservich is a gent. Whatever he does, he never breaks the gentleman's code. He may get played with and such, but he always pays top price. He came to England to be a gentleman and a gentleman, an English Gentleman, he remains.'

Geraldine came back in without Mr Tosservich in tow, flashing a ten pound note. She held it up and waved it about. Coming up close to me, she held up the tenner in my face.

'See cuntface! I've got instant money on call. What you got to offer?'

'An anus?'

She scoffed.

'It's my anus, not yours, he's after.'

'Did you wash your mouth out?'

Now she went up to Mr Crikey and started to run her hands over him.

'Your boss said I've got to give you the full mouth treatment.'

He laughed and smiled and sweated. She put her hand in his inside pocket and after a few seconds located his wallet. She took two tenners out of his wallet and disappeared out the back pulling Mr Crikey with her. I watched the pair go, not enjoying things. One of the big breasted women pulled me to her so we sat close together as if we were going to burst into a tango. I ran my hand over her breasts and she kissed me hard and pushed her tongue deep into my mouth. When we broke off she went at my request and got me a large whiskey with one piece of ice. She came back. I drank the whiskey and began to feel different. And the difference was growing on me. The woman whispered in my ear.

'Your friend might wear her mouth out here.'

'She's no friend of mine. We just got a job together. With the old fat man.'

'He escape death many time.'

'I hear.'

'He got a right to be a fool and a fat man.'

I got up and staggered towards the door and up the stairs to the street. I knew the streets. I had been a butchers boy to the Queen's Butchers. This was my manor. I went to school around the corner. I slept rough here. I ran from the police for three months and lived rough here. Now I was drunk here. I would have to find a *hole to hole up in.* I staggered down streets and ended up looking into the window of the John Sandoe Bookshop in Blacklands Terrace. I now remembered a young woman who had taken me in four years before. I staggered across the street and rang the top bell. Vanessa came down the stairs. And she looked at me and laughed and giggled and four years disappeared. In a flash.

But I imagined it. When I did ring the bell an old woman came to the door and told me to go away and there was no Vanessa living there. And there had not been a Vanessa living there. And she had lived there for ten years.

How could I get home now I was so drunk? There seemed only one course open to me and that was to find a place to sleep. I had fallen. I was 19 and fallen. I would have to find a place to just sit and be sick.

Soon I was sick, wretchedly, in the street. Then I fell down and got up and

everything was clear. I would go back to my room I shared with Karen. And I would confess my stupidity. And then I would sleep and the next morning go off to *London Night,* to sell advertising. The next morning I got to the magazine late. Geraldine was already sitting on her desk, not at it, talking in a sultry voice to someone who she knew needed advertising.

'I think I better come and see you and talk this out face to face. Shall I come to your restaurant?'

She giggled. Giggling, I realised, was her way of communicating. It saved words.

She put the phone down and looked at me.

'So what happened to you last night, you little drunken skunk?'

'You don't need to know people long before you're talking to them as if you've known them for ever.'

She came up close. Her face was alive. She was well dressed in a suit, with her large breasts pushing forward.

'I like you, fuck features. So I am

going to take you for a coffee and we are going to plan a campaign that means soon we'll be rolling in it.'

'I love you.'

'I know you love me. I knew it when you looked at me first. You saw me as I really am. Let's get out of here before the fat man arrives.'

'Have you always been so rude?'

'Since I was five. Maybe before. Let's get out of here.'

We met the fat man on the stairs with Crikey.

'Strategy meeting, Mister Tosseroff. Morning.'

We slid past them. Out in the street, a warm Soho day in mid summer, she took my arm. And led me to the Patisserie Valerie. At one stage she ran her hand over my arse and smiled at me.

'I want every bit of you, mate.'

Black hair, red lips, mad eyes, and full mad mouth. And purely curved.

'You are a fucking heavy bird. I've never known anyone on the make like you.'

'You should meet my mum. And that tosser my dad. I've going to be having a cappacine. Have you heard of one?'

'Frothy coffee. I had a girlfriend who bought me one but ate all the froth off.'

'Then she was a cunt. That's the best part.'

We sat and she put out a hand and took mine.

'I like you. As soon as I saw you. But are you John or Paul?'

'I had my look before the Beatles came along.'

'But you were no one. Now girls look at you and they hope you have some of the luck of the Beatles in you. So they want to get you into bed.'

'You talk like a bloke.'

'And you talk like a girl.'

'That's what's happening, the girls are become blokes.'

'And the blokes are becoming girls. I'm having fun.'

'So am I.'

'But you've got a bird already. Haven't you? I can tell.'

'I've got a bird. Yes.'

'That doesn't bother me.'

We drank our coffees and Geraldine just talked about what she wanted to do. And no, she didn't suck anyone off. She just led them along and got their money. 'You suck em and they've got you. They've had you. No, you have to string them along and fuck off before it gets too serious. I'm just loud.'

A clock struck and I had a feeling that I could sit here all day talking to Geraldine, whether holding my hand or not. I felt tranquil. Geraldine wanting me made me feel happy. After failing to get into art school for the new year I was fucked. I did not work hard enough. I had given up the hard work to be with my girlfriend. And now I was suffering the defeat. The biggest defeat, worse than being locked up again. I was now defeated completely. I had lost everything I had been, or was becoming. Now I would have nothing to show for it. So sitting and forgetting the tragedy of my life, with Geraldine, was a holiday from neglectfulness.

Why had I worked so obdurately from leaving Reformatory to getting into art school? And then worked so hard there for the first term? Until I met my serious girlfriend and then got love struck, and fell out with my studies and efforts. Art became second to love. As I sat looking at Geraldine, I knew I would have put the same passion into her. As my father said very early on in my life, I was 'Cuntstruck'.

We sat for over an hour and planned nothing.

'I like being with you. Shall we go back to my place?'

'We need to make money.'

'We can start tomorrow.'

'If I go back to your place it'll be drinking and fucking.'

'Do you take me for a girl like that?'

'Where are you from?'

'The Isle of Grain.'

'Scotland?'

'No, you cunt, just beyond London in Kent.'

She held both of my hands as if we were a partnership. She was good to be with and look at. But even I knew that she could turn my life upside-down. And I was with one girl. And that seemingly was enough.

'I'll draw you but not fuck you.'

'Why would you want to draw me?'

'Because I could make you look sexy and desirable, Because you are. Then we could make them into prints and sell them on the Portobello Road.'

'And we wouldn't have to work for the fat man? What about your girlfriend?'

'I think she's stuck with me. She wants out.'

'Do you?'

'I'm trying to imagine life without her. It's hard. I think she is the first true love I ever had.'

'You're not going to start crying are you?'

'Not in front of you. But I'll draw you.'

We were playing around. We had to get out and sell ads, but we would rather sit in the Patisserie Valerie in Old Compton Street. And talk shit with each other. I imagined drawing her. She would have been a great model. But then I would have had to fuck her. And then I would have got into trouble, and weakened love for my girl.

I needed to live somewhere where I could be with a few girls. Get some money from maybe pouncing. And living only for drawing and painting; as I had the year before.

My first client was a Greek gentleman with a restaurant in Queensway. I called in and he looked at the magazine and said disparaging things about it. I said it was getting better all the time. He said that if I wrote a review of his restaurant he would take an ad. I said that would be alright but could we do it the other way round. He buy the ad and then I would get the review written. He sat me down at a table and smiled at me.

'Write the review yourself. I give you lunch now.'

It was 2pm. I was hungry.

'You have good meal. You write review and I take ad.'

I was very hungry. He brought out stuffed vine leaves and dips. We began. I started to eat as he told me about how difficult it was to be a Greek coming to London in 1946 with no money and no prospects. He kept calling for more food as I finished the course. And he gave me red wine. I had about three glasses and felt good. I proposed to him I did a drawing for him. And put it up on the wall.

'You can do that boy. Of a naked lady?'

'Yes. A very naked lady.'

He smiled and laughed and got interested in the idea.

'You draw naked ladies?'

'I do. There's a girl who works selling ads. I'm going to be drawing her. You can have a picture on the wall. But you have to buy an ad for a month. No, two months.'

His eyes seemed to be made wider by the thought that I drew naked women.

'I go to strip shows. Nothing. Titivate. That's all they do. But to draw naked lady.'

'You could have a naked lady in your restaurant. And I could draw her. And your diners could watch me.'

I was too drunk now, having added to the three glasses. So I just got up and walked down into Kensington Gardens and found a tree to sleep under. My first day at selling ads for *London Night* had produced a slim chance that I might get an ad from the Greek man. But it was slim. But he might buy a good drawing of Geraldine.

When I woke up it was a warm evening and I felt guilty. Karen would have been waiting for me. I looked at my watch. It was 8.30. I was a wretch. I was a piece of shit. Would I ever get back to how I was in 1964? When all that I needed was art and the chance to make it?

You had to be single minded. If you wanted to make art. I could not be. I would combine many things with making art; and that would mean that I would never be in the next generation of artists. I was a failure, as I walked across the park to the Kensington side; to Karen, who would be waiting for me.

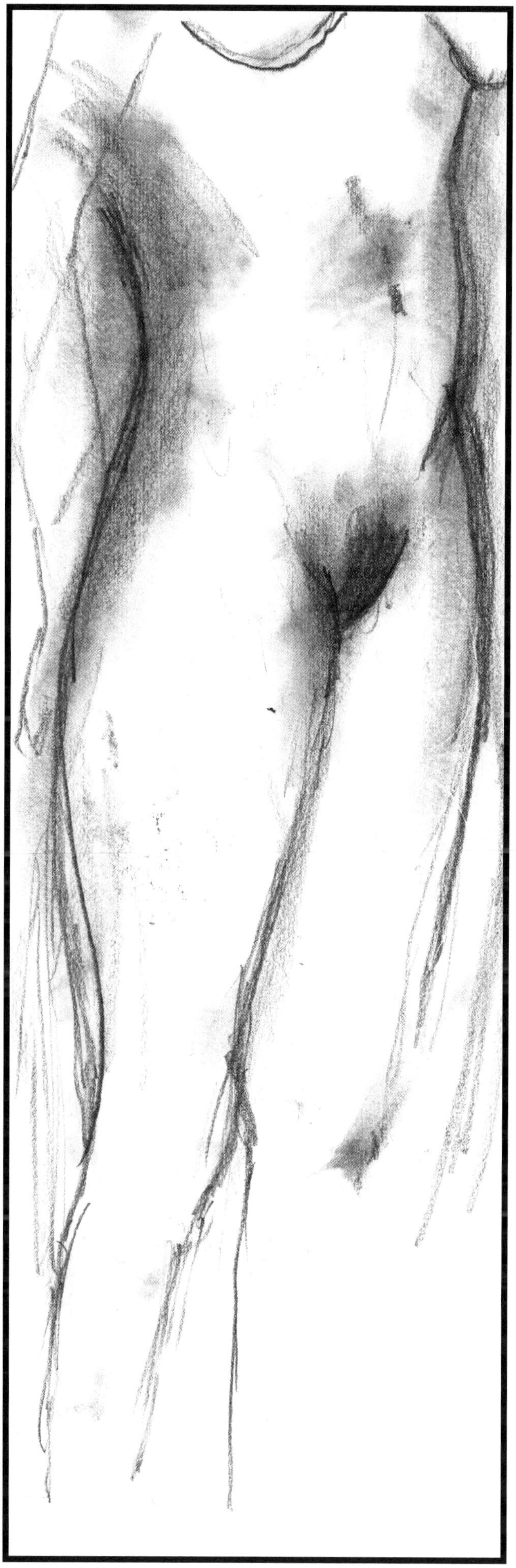

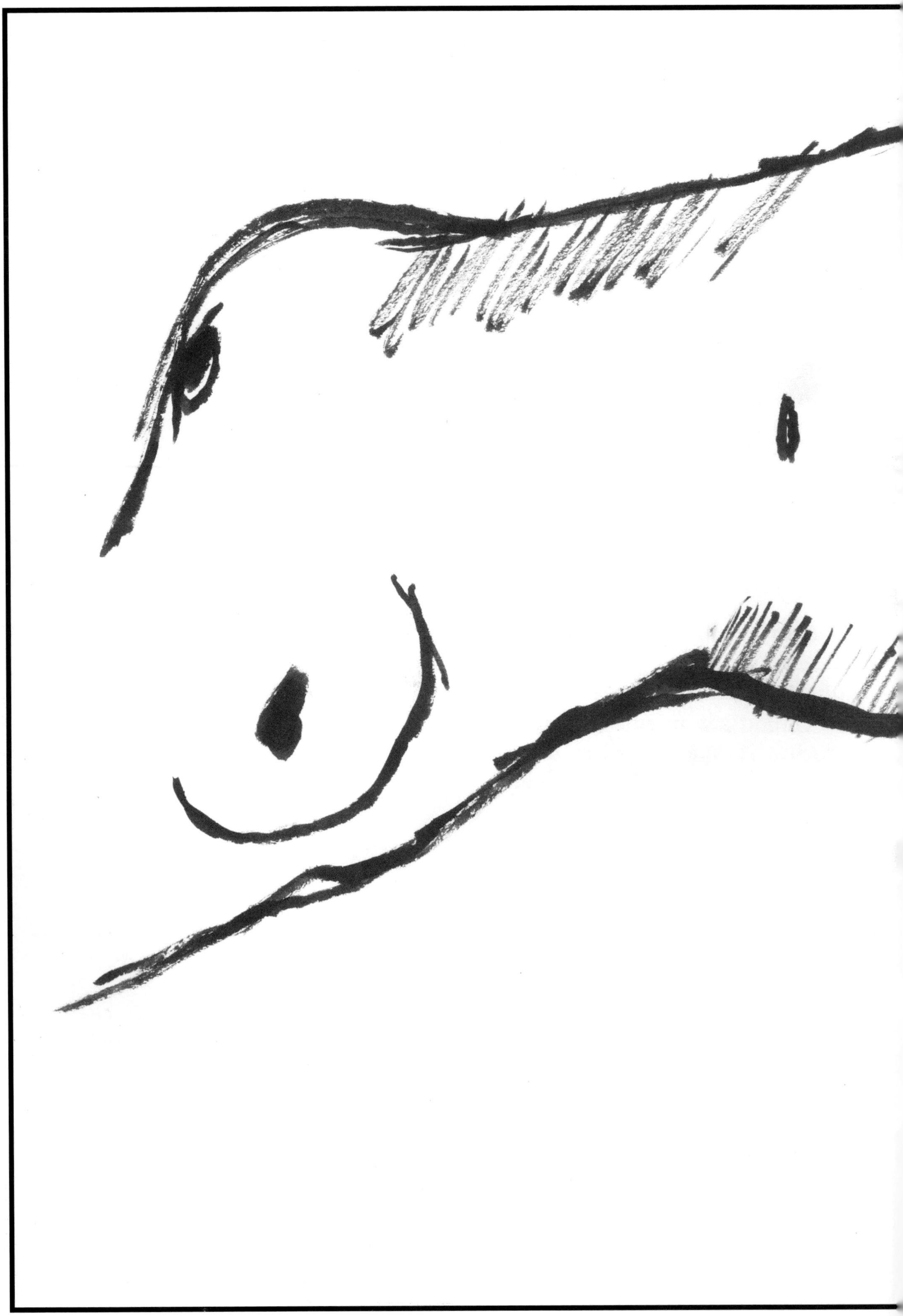

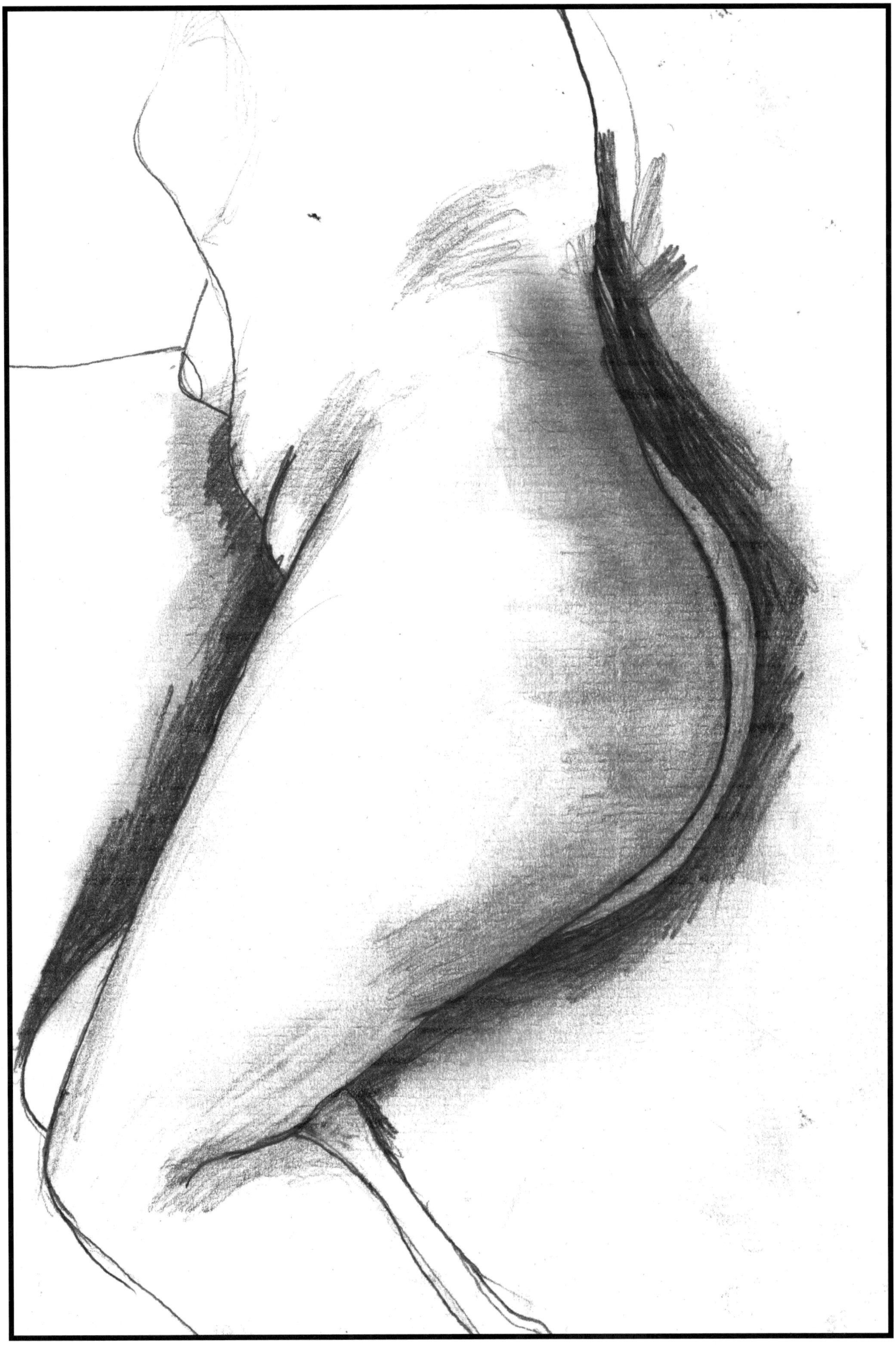

Paris. 1967.

She cried as I undressed her. The wind blew the slight, dirty laced curtain back in my small window, revealing Sacre Coeur on the hill above us.

'Imagine, Jean, what it is like when your mind is revolutionary and your body is reactionary. That is my predicament. I am reactionary in appearance.'

I carried on undressing her. I was down to her corset, suspenders and stockings. As I removed another piece of garment she displayed red marks all over her midrift. Now removing the corset meant getting her to stand again. I pulled it off, undoing stays that I had never known existed. Down to her small, neat, fine filigreed knickers; I could see the full charm of her. The red marks on her showed how she had penned herself in. A perfectly formed, big-breasted, good-arsed girl of seventeen.

'Do I fuck you first or draw you first?'

'You don't even listen. I am a thing to be used.'

'I think the drawing should be first.'

'What do you care about my tears Jean? What do they mean to you?'

Now she stood un-knickered, and bra off. Only her suspenders and stockings on. I was full of admiration. Tall, but biggish.

Long blonde hair, mixed with red. Skin like porcelain with a suggestion of a summer holiday or two. Whited areas where her bikini covered the cunt and arse area and the tit area. A perfectly made French girl from a place called Alsace Lorraine that meant nothing to me.

'I don't comment because I don't know what the hell you are going on about. Revolutionary head? Reactionary body? Monique, I am English. I come from a small island. What are you talking about?'

She sat back in the chair and cried big tears now. Not tears of embarrassment as I undressed her for the first time. Which is how I read her first tears. But big tears with deep breaths and distress. I embraced her.

'I am sorry, Monique. I thought you were a bit frightened of this.'

It took her a few minutes to be able to talk again. I waited holding her, the most perfectly formed girl I had seen in all my life. English girls seemed to hide themselves in bad underwear. Art students, of which I knew many, did not change their knickers. They did not play with their bodies. And they did not trim their bushes. Janet, a recent one, needed serious attention, but she did not do any of the things you would hope.

But beautiful Monique was golden looking and neatly trimmed, overwhelming the gardening metaphors. Revealing the lips of her undercarriage rather than swaddling them in hair. And now she was crying about the difference between body and mind. And I, a one-time art student who knew all there was to know about most art, knew nothing about the crisis of reaction and revolution; not quite understanding the way she used the words.

To me, Paul Cezanne was the greatest of all revolutionaries. For he overthrew the rules of Western perspective and the Salon; even rubbing Impressionism's nose into the dirt. Picasso with Cubism did the same a bit later, building on Cezanne. But political reaction and revolution? I knew only names: Lenin, Marx, Hitler. But Monique, seventeen, at the Berlitz studying German and English off the Boulevard Haussmann and learning piano and other things I could not fathom, knew all about this stuff.

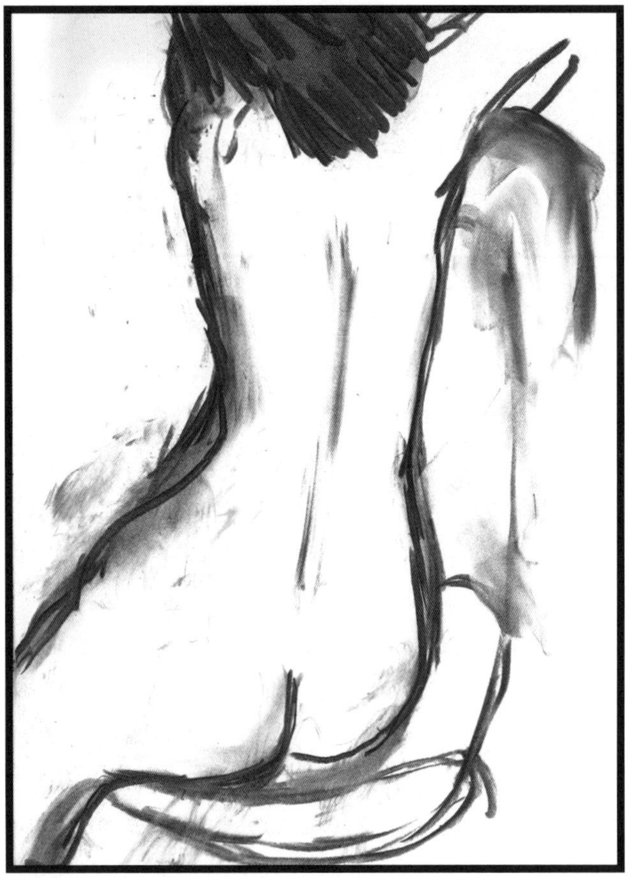

I knew that Trotsky got an ice pick in his head from Stalin. I knew Hitler had taken drugs and shot himself in the head. And then had his body burned with kerosene. I knew that because my mate Brain worked it out that I was his reincarnation. That I was born at the end of January 1946 and Hitler topped himself in April 1945. Brain said, 'Well Bird, you little cunt. The old cunt was leaving the world with a flame, while your mum and dad were fucking each other silly on a slum bed in slummy Notting Hill. You are definitely the spirit of the old cunt; even down to the fact that you are both shit painters. Artists without a drop of talent.'

Brain, had got some education. I got my education in the boys' prison and reformatory system. Brain would never accept I was little more than a piece of post-war social shit, a poor statistic of the underclass, lower down the social scale than even his modest beginnings. Brain was poetic in his condemnations of me and what he called my opportunism. He would, though, have punctured big holes in Monique's understanding of Reaction and Revolution. He knew about History.

'Tell me what you mean by this, Monique. I want to understand.'

She dried her tears on my shirt, and blew her nose on my handkerchief. She laughed and smiled.

'Sorry Jean. You run away from the police in London to get away. And you run into me. Depressed because my body does not match my mind.'

'Tell me what the problem is. Then we can get on with the other stuff.'

She slapped me lightly on the face.

'Your hair is better than a girl's, Jean. Such curls. You have hair of the *Ancien Regime.* That is alright for boys to have such hair. But me, Jean: I have the body of the *Ancien Regime.* My mind is full of Marxism and Jean Paul Sartre, and Simone de Beauvoir. But I do not have the body of revolution. The slim with no breasts. A small derriere. More like a boy than a girl. That is the body of today, Jean. But me; me. I have the body of the days before the French Revolution. Before the *Sans Cullotes* stormed the

Bastille and ended the old oppression. I have the body of a mistress of one of the Louis. All ass, as you would say. All ass and tits.'

Now she laughed at herself. I lit two Gauloises Disque Bleu, my favourite of all cigarettes. Monique had showed me how to tear the soft top of the packet so only one at a time came out, and not tear back the whole top. I was pleased with this small improvement in the quality of my understanding. I passed one to her and she took a deep deep breath and blew out the wonderful smoke all over my face. When she smoked like this she put me to shame. I was a recent convert to cigarettes, never smoking when I was inside. Never smoking until a year before. I sat with her and held her hand. My erection which came while undressing her had gone somewhere else. I realised that I had to listen to her to get to the drawing and the fucking. The drawing would open her up. It had to come first.

'Last year Jean, I realised the impediment of my body. When we went to Munich with my ecole. Fourteen girls we were and we went to the *Alterpinarketeke* gallery of paintings. I was looking at Madame Pompadour painted by Boucher The biggest dress you could see, overflowing the painting. Almost, I thought, coming out of the painting. When I heard the girls giggling. They called me over to the next painting. It was another Francois Boucher. I will always remember the title of that painting Jean. *Le Derriere de la Mamazelle O'Murphy.* They were giggling because they saw a young girl laying on her front, sitting up. With her naked bum. And the young girl, and even the bum, was me! I had been captured Jean, over 200 hundred years ago. By the court painter to Louis the XVth, almost the last Louis before the revolution. And the girls laughed and laughed and I suffered mortification Jean. My soul broke within me.'

The telling of the story cheered her up. She had a smile.

'So you have an old body? But you want to be skinny like an English model.'

I said this with an obvious dislike. I hated the new thin woman. I wanted tits and arses. I wanted firm bodies. To draw and to fuck. I did not want to be fucking boys with bodies like Peter Pan. I wanted Monique. And Monique was the apex, the apotheosis of all that was beautiful about a woman in the 20th century.

'I want to be like Simone de Beauvoir, Jean. Jean Paul Sartre would never look at a woman with a body like me. He would believe that with a body like mine I would not be on the side of the revolution. And the call to unite the workers of the world to overthrow their masters and exploiters.'

'I see. This is all about style. If you are a red but have a blue body –.'

'Exactement. You have it. If I went down to Flores, to Les Maggots now, and presented myself to Sartre and said, 'I love all of your work. And I love all that you wish to do in the world. I am here to be for your use. You know what he would say?'

'What?'

'He would not even listen to me.

He would have a quizzical face as he surveyed my giant glands, and my big ass. And my big smiling face with lips so big and alluring. I would be the old face. I would be the reminder of the exploitation of the *Ancien Regime.* Because I would not be slim and thin, and boylike like Simone.'

'So you want to be modern. And look like some waif. Some bit of bird. I see. And this cunt Sartre.'

'He is no cunt, Jean. He is the finest man on the earth. He puts his whole life before the poor. He gives everything.'

'But he only wants to fuck boys, dressed as girls.'

She shouted.

'No. Fuck you, Jean. Don't say this about my hero. He is not a reactionary. Like you are. You like my body. You love my body. You admire my body. You want to draw it and fuck it. Why? Because I shall tell you: because you are a reactionary. Blacks and Jews you say fuck the world. Those poison thoughts you bring to Paris. You are reactionary so you like a body from the *Ancien Regime.* Of course you would.'

I was lost with this girl. This middle class girl. With the best of all arses. Sitting there, with only her stockings and suspenders. Which added to the beauty of her. What could I say? I would have to find a way out of this intellectual shit. She did not know about Paul Cezanne. And I knew nothing about Jean Paul Sartre.

'Of course you are right, Monique. But don't you understand, I got out of London to become a better person. I wanted to get rid of prejudice. That is why you mean so much to me. You are changing me. At this very moment, I am thinking of all the good Jews I have known in my life. All the blacks who have been kind to me. I would not be doing that without you.'

She laughed.

'I love the word 'scum'. I learned that last year when I was at language school in Brighton. The shit that rises to the top of the dirty bath water. Jean, you are scum. Underclass, *Lumpen Proletariat* as we Marxists call you kind of people. You are the piece of shit on the shoe of British Imperialism.'

She was smiling.

'Monique, if I become a Marxist, can I fuck you and draw you?'

She looked at me very carefully.

'I can sense your devotion to me, Jean. I undress with you. I know you see some gift wrapping coming off some perfect form. I love the feeling you give me. I know you want to enter me, and draw me. That is, for a boy like you from London, that is a tres tres compliment. Yes. I will make you a Marxist.'

'Now?'

'This is not like Holy Communion, Jean. Or baptism. You cannot become a Marxist like you become a catholic. You go to church and you pray. We have no religion in our Marxism. But I will try and take you there. You must work on your imperialistic hatings. The hate of Europe for the poor world. You must take some study to understand.'

I drew Monique laying like the Boucher at the Munich gallery. I knew the painting. I knew Boucher. As I drew her I thought about all the good blacks and Jews I knew. I thought about Mr Tosservich who had survived the Warsaw Ghetto. And got to England and bought slum houses in Notting Hill. And sold industrial chocolate and second hand clothes and got them fixed up new. Who desperately, committedly, turned his hand to all things to do with making money. Who probably knew no other way of living. That making money was like being a farmer. Or a gardener. You had to keep growing stuff. You could never stop. And the same with the now dead Mr Tosservich. Died of something with the heart. As I applied a B3 pencil to some fine paper I bought at an art shop on the Boulevard St Michael in the *Quartier Latine,* getting the utter softness, the inspiring softness of Monique's bare arse, I thought of the tragedy of Mr Tosservich. And how *London Night* petered out a few months after we went to work for him. But how he seemed to have moved on to the next thing. To do with second hand furniture painted in bright Union Jack colours. And selling it on the Portobello Road. That was the last time I saw Mr Tosservich. Making money doing things that other people were doing. But him doing it with a bigger warehouse and more stock. The Jew beating others. And sowing hate for himself in his trail. A man not made well-mannered by life.

I did not talk when drawing. The clean undercarriage, bereft of the hair of old England, shown completely. Lips and anus meeting together. I felt my soul rise to my mouth. I felt that God was talking to me when I drew her cunt from behind, laying as she was on her front and half sitting up. I knew the painting she saw at Munich in reproduction. The library at Chelsea School of Art showed many good books on art of that period.

Mr Tosservich smiled at me across the previous two years. For a while he worked on Portobello Road. I saw him there standing by an enormous wardrobe made in the war, done in shit wood and in a standard style. You could sell a lot of old chests of drawers because they were small and manageable; if you painted them with Union Jacks and bright *'Swinging London'* colours. But a wardrobe with a big Union Jack spread all over its giant form: that looked dumb. Mr Tosservich standing beside it looked stupid. He offered me it for a fiver. I said I had nowhere to live. I was sleeping on sofas. He said he had a nice sofa. And then he went into his warehouse to see if there was a deal coming, even from me, ushering me in after him. I turned and walked off down towards The Tabernacle to see my Aunt who lived opposite. Where would I put a sofa if I had no room? The post-war triumph of the Allies over Hitler had unravelled for me. And Mr Tosservich was to die within a few months.

Monique lay and fell asleep and I carried on drawing her. I drew softly. I managed to capture the softness with the pencil and was pleased with how well she modelled. How much she enjoyed being drawn. I took a break, lit up a Galouises Disque Bleu and sat and looked at her. The little net curtain blew in this late Summer's day. And Monique to slip into a deeper sleep. A troubled girl who would never be slim but would be well made.

And would not fit in with the 'style' that you needed to have if you were to be considered 'modern', and 'revolutionary.' When she woke it was too late and she had to rush for some piano lessons. I tried to plead with her that we only had completed part of the deal. But she had to go and said I should have woken her. She rushed out of my room and I fell on the bed despondent and wishing that I had not come to Paris and met with a revolutionary like Monique. I took up my pack of cigarettes and went and sat in the café in Barbes and had a boiled egg and a beer and then another beer. I felt better but could not wait to complete the engagement with Monique. Back at the room I looked at the drawings and cursed my lost chance. And all this history stuff and the tears about not being thin. What shit thinking was this?

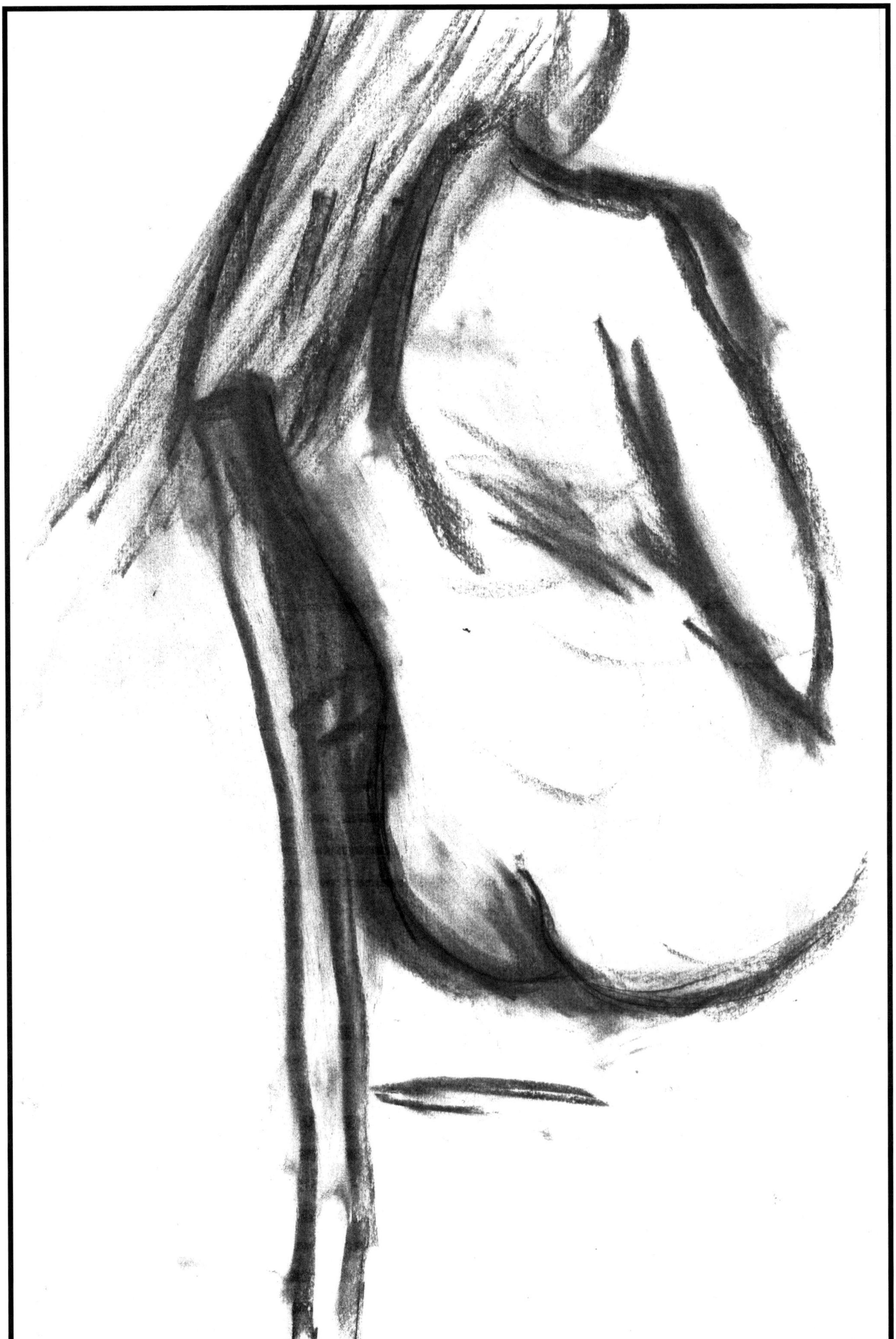

New England. 1980.

Paddy was sick on me. I had given him the salt tablet and he threw his breakfast up all over me. We had just celebrated his fifth birthday and there might have been some cake from the night before. But I lay on the floor of the hotel room as Paddy stood beside me being sick.

It was the salt tablet that had done the damage. Otherwise he was well. Brain started to complain, sitting on his bed as I lay on the floor stretching my back.

'Can't you do that in the bathroom?'

He jumped up off the bed, angry with the smell of sick.

'Fuck off Brain. He can't help it.'

'Well you fucking clean it up.'

He stalked off out. Paddy now smiled, happy that he had the salt tablet out on the floor, and on me.

'Don't worry about Brain, son. He's a cunt.'

'That's £300 you owe.'

'As much as that?'

I was fined every time I swore. It started off at ten pence a swear, but now it seemed to go up by pounds.

Paddy was remarkably clear of vomit. The floor and me had taken the brunt. I got him reading on our bed and cleaned myself up, and then the floor. I finished off my back stretching exercises and then we went out for a walk.

Provincetown in August was full of families and gays. The hotel was mixed. The owners told me that they were Republican, Reagan-loving gays. I was astonished. I had only met left or liberal leaning gays before.

'How can you be gay and rightwing?'

They laughed.

'With incredible difficulty.'

We walked out onto the porch of the clapboard hotel and the sun was brighter than I had ever remembered. This was my first trip to America. We had been here two days. We had headed north from New York in a dark blue Pontiac that had pristine white leather insides. It had 17 miles on the clock when I got into the rented car. It was automatic and no one had explained to me the way to drive something I had never driven before. I used two feet instead of one. We bumped along the roads going north, and it took me a day to realise that you only needed one foot to operate the car. That you kept your other foot tucked up out of the way.

'I'm hungry, Dad.'

'I'm not surprised. Shall we go back to the pancake place?'

'Could we, Dad?'

He had just turned five and I was very worried in America. So many bad stories had been put around about the lack of safety. When we arrived we had got the bus to the train from Kennedy airport. And a police officer, gunned up, sat in each one of the carriages and talked to the passengers. Telling us all to go straight to our destinations. As it was gone midnight all the nuts would be out prowling around.

I held Paddy close to me. Brain kept telling me I was neurotic. I kept telling him to go fuck himself. I had a boy with me. My son. And that was different than being a single grown man.

At the pancake house there was the same waitress called Sharn who the night before had made a fuss of

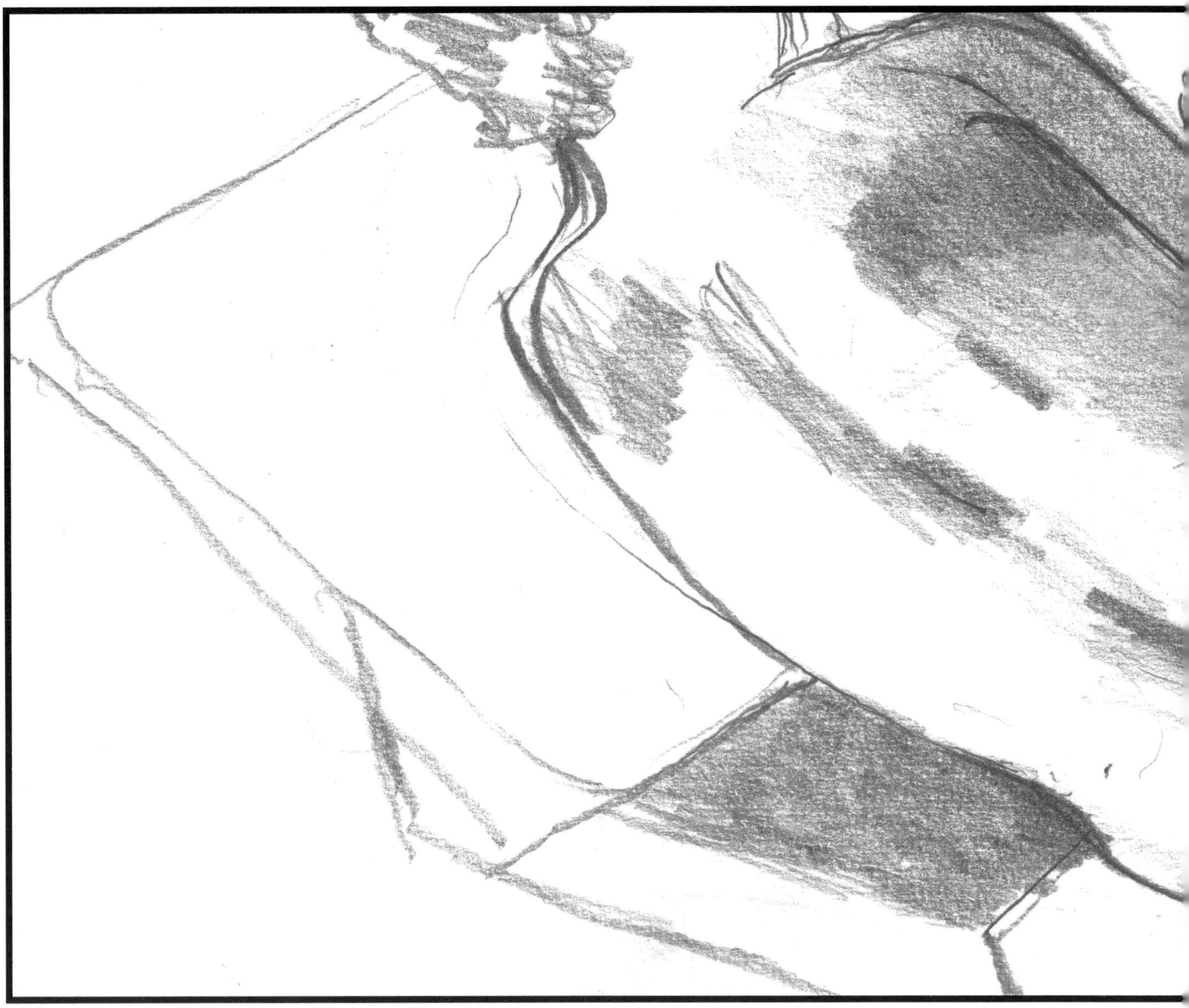

Paddy and me. She had asked us back to her little home which was right by the beach. She had her niece and nephew staying with her. She was an art student from Boston and was up for the summer to work. She had large hair, something that was peculiar to North America at the time. How she got so much hair on her head, and kept it remarkably in place, and not shedding on her customers was a surprise.

We took a seat in the quite dark interior of the café and she came over.

'Good to see you guys. Are you coming over this evening?'

'We are.'

'That'll be great. So what do you want now?'

Paddy wanted a pancake with jam on it. I ordered a coffee and a roll. We sat quietly, looking around at the big meals that seemed to be had by all, irrespective of the size of the person. Everything was big in America, it seemed.

'I so loved meeting you guys.'

'We loved it also.'

We had the pancake and roll and coffee.

Paddy had a large glass of orange juice and then we started to draw on the paper provide by Sharn. I gave him some of my pencils and the waitress gave him crayons. He drew with great dedication. I took out my sketchbook and began to draw the

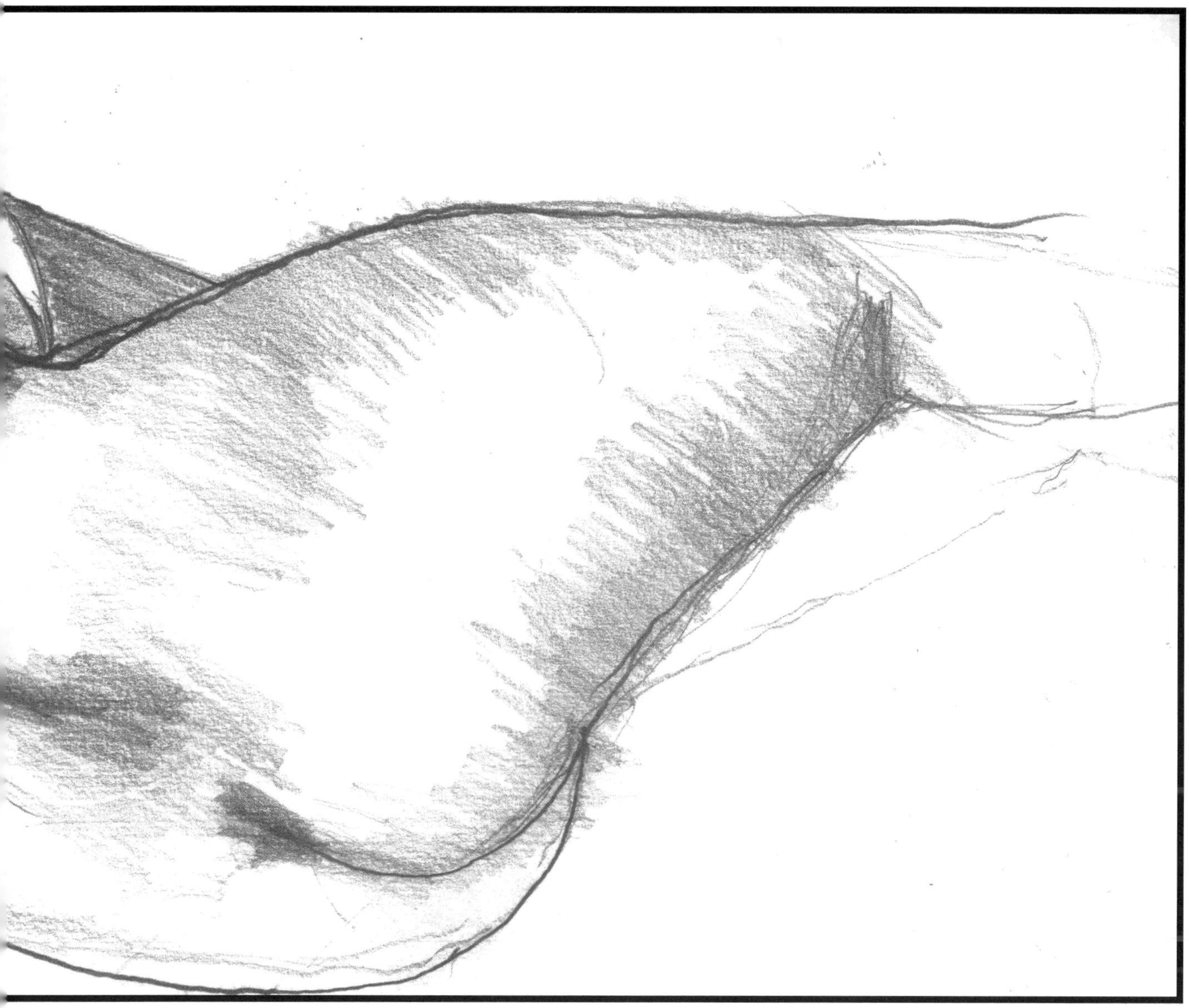

interior. I did it quickly and firmly and was soon pleased with the result. I quickly sketched in people before they moved and laid out tables, loaded with plates. The darkness, with occasional pools of light, made one feel that the season outside, bright and intensive, was somewhere else. We were not in hot Cape Cod on a hot day in August.

Brain came in with a smile. He always smiled when he had made an arse of himself. It was his way of saying sorry. Something that he never did. He sat and had a coffee and looked pleased to be around. I gave him a map to look at while I carried on drawing. The waitress came over and I introduced Brain. Brain had been watching TV the night before so he had not met our new friend. When she walked away Brain said what he always said about women:

'Why do they take an instant fancy to me?'

'Because you are irresistible. Charm mixed with looks. And your innate ability to mesh with female humanity.' Then I laughed. Brain was a cunt.

We left the café with details of where to go to that night. We went back and got ready for a day by the beach. Brain was transfixed with his power to get women, suggesting that come the night he would be 'up' her, as he said. I reserved judgement on the power of his sexual chemistry.

That night we drove over to the little house by the water. The beach was like the garden of the house. And we played and ate and drank. Sharn did not quite understand some of Brain's comments, and his humour. She looked confused when he got too friendly, and pulled herself away. In the kitchen Sharn asked me:

'Is your friend alright?'

'He suffers from a delusion.'

'Delusion? What particular kind?'

'That all women are sexually drawn to him.'

She made a strange face.

'Has he never heard of lesbians?'

'Probably.'

'He better wise up. Some lesbians don't quite go for the male thing.'

'Shall I let him know?'

'Let him find out.'

Sharn and I sat talking about drawing. Paddy raced around wildly with the boy and girl who were twice his age and more. They ran along the beach, played a strange form of sand-castle building that involved more water than sand. And Brain sat watching TV, drinking beers. There was a kind of contentment. But I knew that the beers might not be doing Brain well.

Sharn looked at a sketchbook I had brought with me. I had not drawn since I arrived. She marvelled over the fact that some of the drawings were careful.

'We don't really do the drawing thing. I wish I could.'

'Shall I draw you?'

'Why not?'

We went into her bedroom and she took off her top and her shorts and there she was. One minute she was dressed and the next she was naked.

Her body was healthier looking than my ordinary models. Good, deep tanning, and strong. As if she exercised a lot. I asked her but she said she went to the gym once a week and waited tables.

'I'm always working. That's what it is.'

I fell to drawing her. I did a rough sketch of her large hair. She was trimmed to nothingness below. I sketched and then started a fresh more detailed study. And she lay, like the Naked Maja, the slashed one by Goya in the National Gallery, often called the Rokeby Venus.

I must have drawn for about half an hour. Then the hysterical running around the house as Paddy and the others got madder. I stopped drawing and Sharn dressed as quickly as she had undressed.

We had gone to Provincetown because of my passion for John Marin, an American painter from the early part of the 20th century. I was fascinated by him, with his strangely modern type of watercolours. To me, America was all about Nature. I had read *Walden's Pond,* by Henry Thoreau, who left civilisation behind and moved into a hut he built in the woods near Concorde.

I had read about New England and its history. So coming to Cape Cod was as if I was encountering American Nature. To draw one of its citizens naked was a great bonus. Later I looked at the drawings and was pleased with one of them in the rapid drawing session. Sharn lay on her back with her arse towards me. It did look very like Goya, but rough and inaccurate.

But passable.

I kept the drawing for many years and only lost it when there was a deluge in a basement I lived in later. Many drawings were destroyed, along with books and clothes. But they meant nothing to me. It was the drawing of Sharn that was particularly important to me. Drawn in charcoal it could not survive the deluge and the laying in water for days until I discovered it.

Paddy and I decided it was time to go. Brain though wanted to stay. Now he was drunk but not stupid. I tried to get him to come. But Sharn said leave him.

'I'll bring him back later.'

'I can wait.'

Brain with his drunken, twisted, almost pompous smile scoffed.

'You just don't like to see someone enjoying themselves, do you?'

'I don't. That's right. Especially you.'

We left. We got back to the hotel and a few hours later Brain arrived back. I had been laying in bed thinking about how I wished I was back in England. And not quite enjoying what was supposed to be my first trip to America. I had dreamed as a child of waking up in our Fulham council flat and looking out of the window. And instead of seeing gas works and coke-yards, seeing skyscrapers and America. Now I was there I could not wait to be home.

Paddy missed his mum and I missed England and I wondered whether I would ever return to America and get used to the place. Sharn, with her fine body, got me thinking about how Americans, simply by being Americans, were different from Europeans. Why? How? I fell asleep before I could resolve the question. And Brain apparently got kissed and fondled, but that he had to reject all offers because he was pissed stupid.

We woke early and headed inland to the Catskill mountains, where we were going to go to a small and strange place that we had spotted on the map called Phoenicia. That sounded about right: to finish this way, one week in America. Hills and cabins and some old historical name. The car was the best thing about the holiday. We booked into a motel and there was a fast-flowing river nearby. I sat on the banks of the river and did some drawings of the trees that dipped into the stream. I looked at the drawings of Sharn and realised that if I kept at it I might catch up again. I might get as good as I had been when I was younger. Brain came and looked at the drawings.

'Crap.'

'Thank you.'

'But you got her arse. I'll say that. Yes, you got that.'

I kept drawing the trees over the water. Then we took a walk up a mountain and I looked forward to getting back. Having a child with me made me feel vulnerable. And Brain was not much help with my vulnerability.

'Trees! For fuck sake.'

That was the last word that Brain said before we came down from the mountain. The car throbbed and purred as we drove back to Phoenica. And in two days we would get back to London. And isolation and separation, and fear for the safety of my child could be a thing of the past.

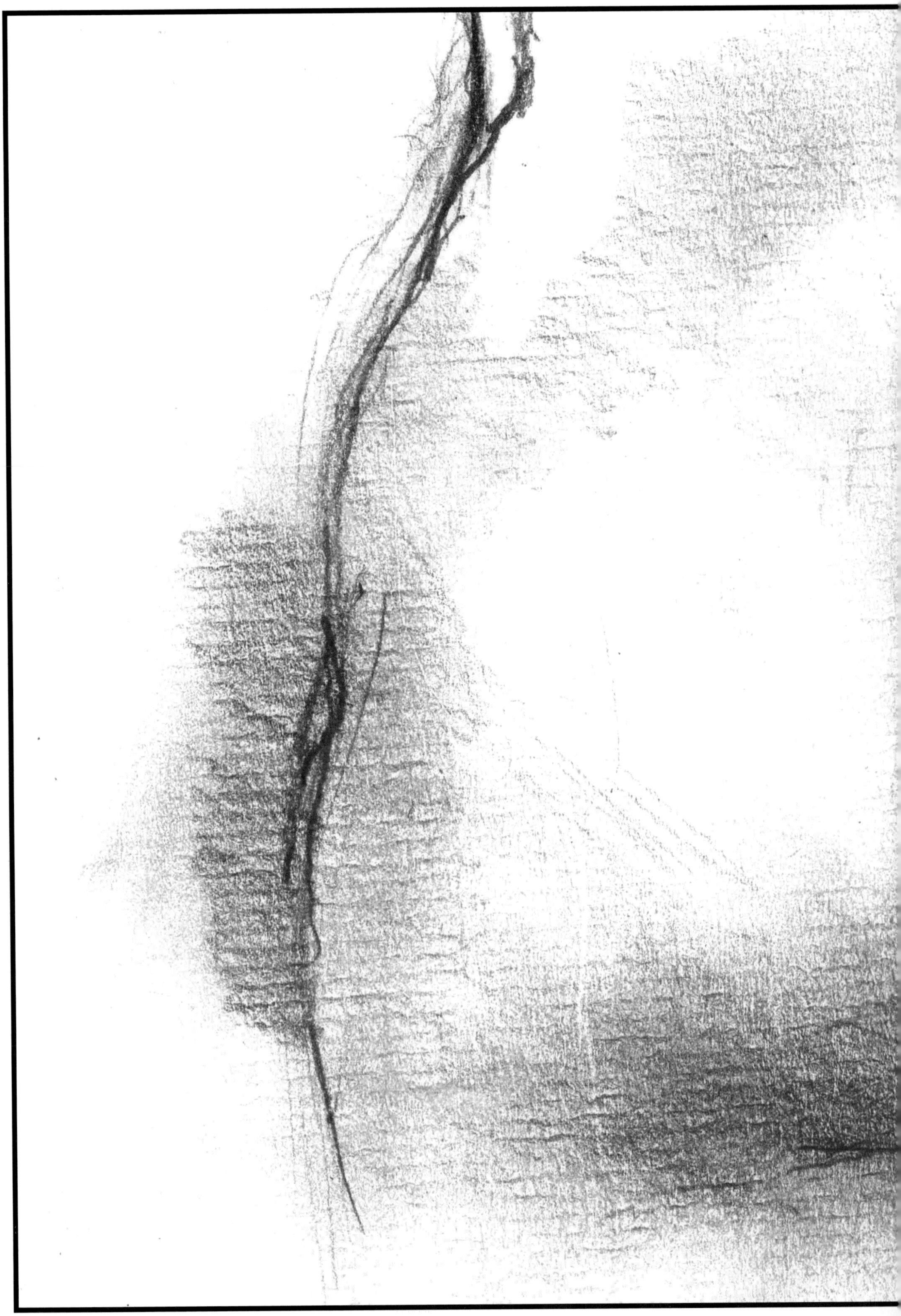

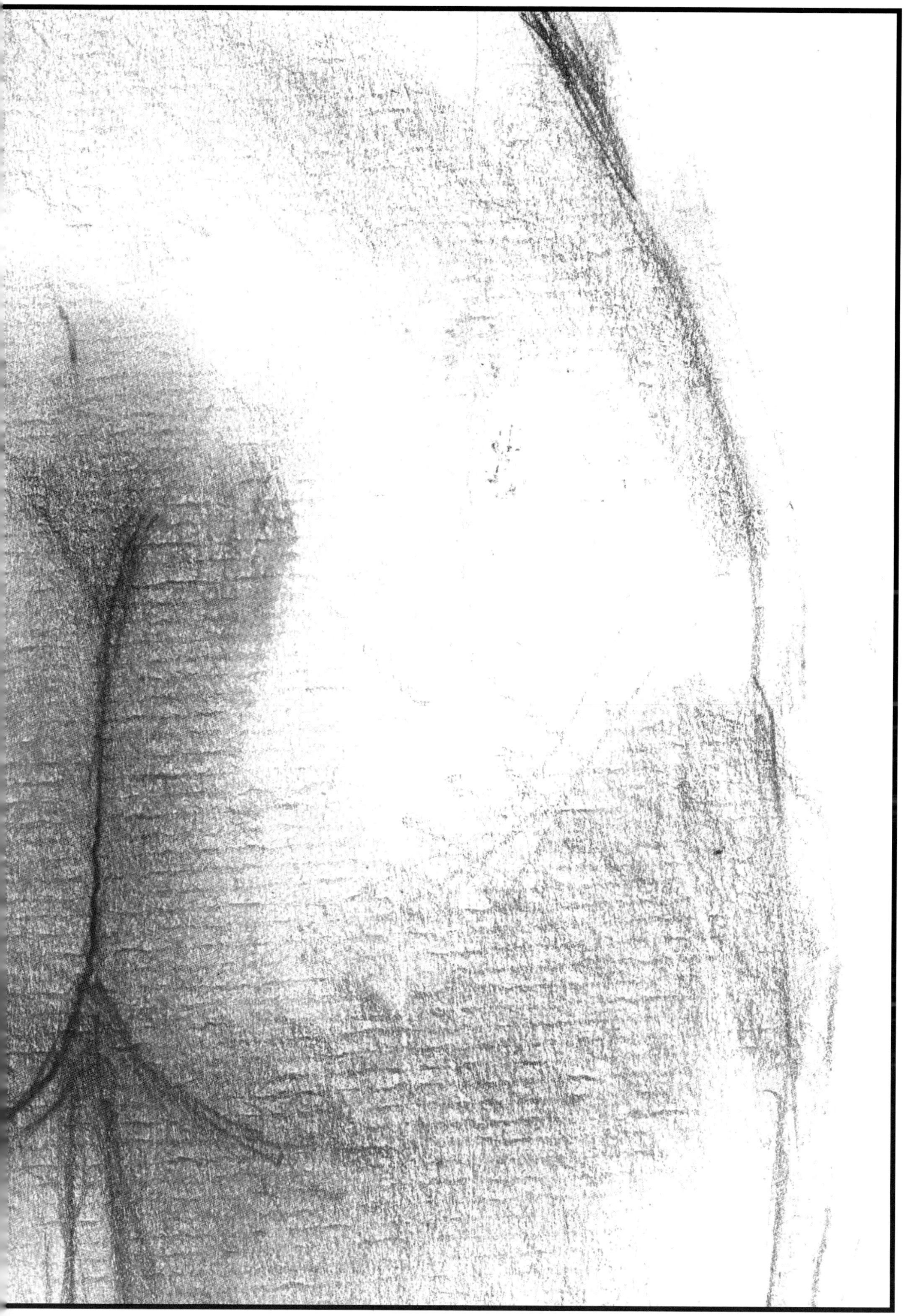

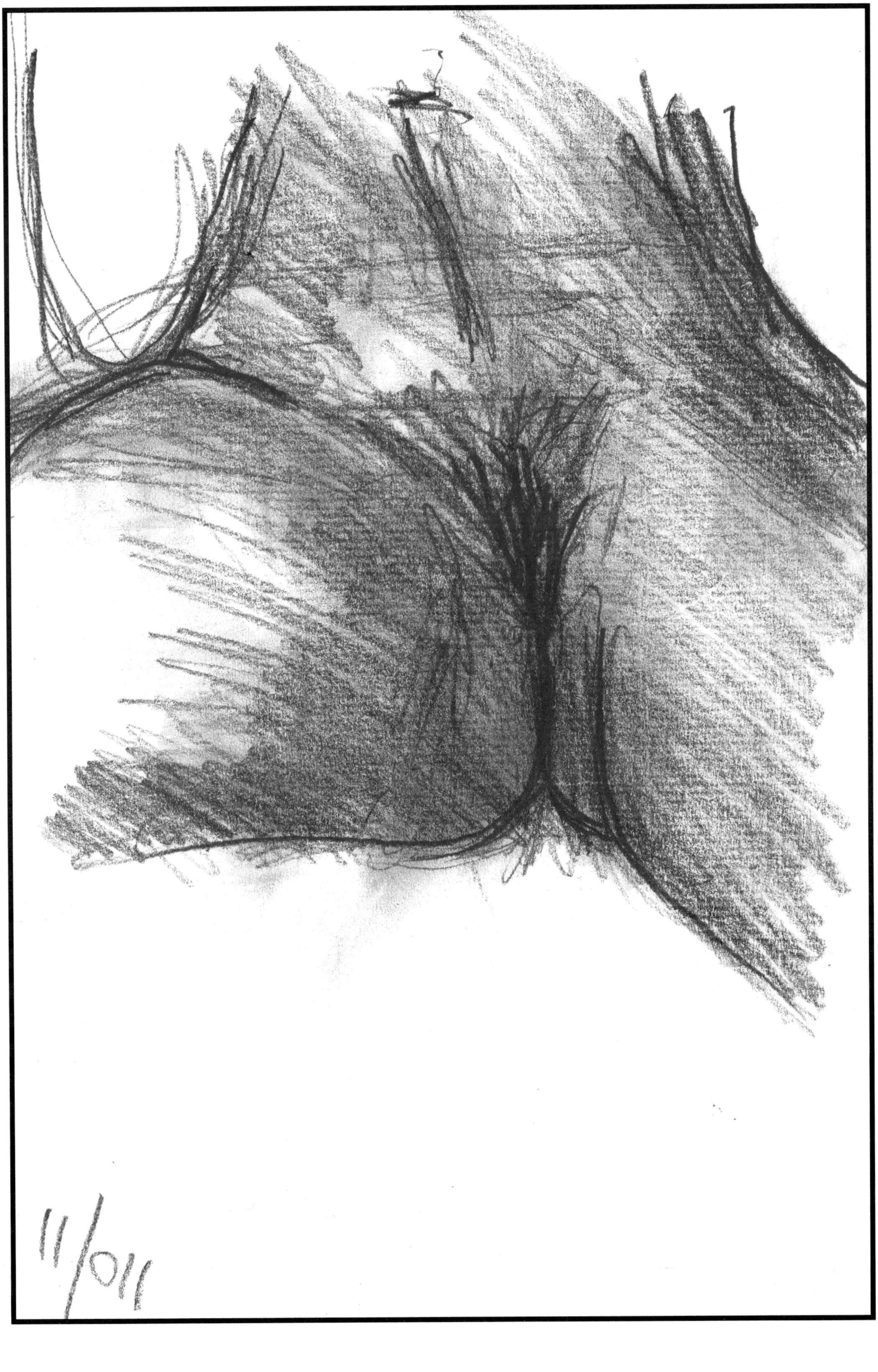
11/011

Notting Hill. 1987.

1987 and I brought Hitler to Notting Hill. Swastikas graced the Gate Theatre, above the Prince Albert public house. Outside of which, three decades earlier, my mother and us boys caught the 28 bus to our incarceration in an orphanage. My play was about idealism. I was in a one-man war with the evils of Idealism. Everyone seemed to live in a world of wishful thinking, of dreaming. And Notting Hill seemed a good place to burst the shit-bubble of idealism. To expose the crime of dreaming, which could lead to consumeristic capitalism, or to Nazism. All relied heavily on wishful thinking and a callous disregard for reality.

But I won't labour the point here. All I'll say is that I was returning to the place of my birth to excoriate the everyday thinking of life, and do it with a play about Hitler's followers after his death.

The night after my Hitler play had finished, I went to a meeting of 'Friends of the Portobello Road'. It was in a small room above the bar of the Sun in Splendour, at the top of Portobello Road. I wanted to hear about history and Notting Hill, a place that I still loved, in spite of the growing gentrification of the place; in spite of the brickbats I had received in it.

A woman was talking about local history and she did very well, telling us about all the little dairies that sprung up in the late 19th century; many of the proprietors coming from Wales. I listened and had a few pints of Guinness, and then a few more. By the end of the talk I was not as clear headed as I was at the start.

I made a comment:

'Most local history is bollocks. Because it doesn't take into account the big events. My grandfather died, and lived in Notting Hill. Not because he had something happen to him in Notting Hill. But because he was a soldier in the trenches in Flanders in the First World War. And he got mustard gas used on him by the Germans.'

Everyone looked around at me, talking from the back. A man stood up and raised his hand.

'We don't allow profanities and swearing in this forum, if you don't mind.'

'Since when is bollocks a profanity or a swear word? Most swear words are just outlawed words from Cromwell's time. I mean, it's not as if I used the 'cunt' word, is it?'

This caused discussion and cries of shame. And people standing up from their collapsible seats and telling me to leave.

'But I only asked a question, members. I didn't even use the 'fuck' word. Only bollocks, which as we know is a common term of description for thinking that does not bear consideration.'

The meeting got awkward and people looked at me as if I was a bad person. They would not listen to my claim that I was entirely innocent and that they were the people with the problems. They suspended the meeting until I was prepared to leave. But I had to make a passing statement.

'I was born here, fellow members. That is, if you will extend membership to me.'

'No way,' shouted a few people.

'I am probably one of the few in this room born here. So I should be listened to. If I promise not to use the 'cunt' word or the 'fuck' word, will you allow me to join?'

You could not hear the last few words, drowned out by a dozen 'shames' and 'get outs'. So I left wishing them all the best, adding that I hoped that they all did not look upon me as a low-life piece of piss and shit.

I went downstairs to the bar, had another Guinness and then stood at the bar complaining about the lack of hospitality of the Friends of the Portobello Road. After the pint I walked out into the street and decided that I would retrace my steps to the Princess Alexandra where earlier I had had my first Guinness of the evening.

'Excuse me.'

I turned around and saw a flaming red-headed woman with green pullover and black jeans. I looked at her expecting more insults from a member, for I had noticed her in the audience.

'No. I won't be paying my membership tonight.'

She walked closer to me.

'You are a brutal and rather nasty person.'

But she said it with a smile.

'I am a rather brutal and nasty person. And you are a Canadian.'

She laughed.

'Get away. How did you know?'

'Your hair. And your green pullover. Only a Canadian would put such two colours together.'

'You lie.'

'I think your accent might have aided my ability to fathom.'

'Where are you going?'

'For a drink at the pub my mum met my dad in, exactly 48 years ago. Would you like to join me?'

'You try and stop me. I have always liked offensive people.'

We walked along. I was high but I was not staggering. I still had my senses about me. I looked at her hair. It stuck up wild in the air, like a red Afro. Wild and running and falling onto her face.

'Belinda.'

'John.'

We shook hands.

We talked about the meeting.

'I liked what you said about local history often not taking into account the big things that were going on.'

'Thank you. I thought long and hard about it. Is that why you followed me out?'

'You seemed to be fun. I am in London for a few days. I haven't had any fun in the last few days, since I got here.'

'Then let the fun commence. Where are you staying?'

'In a B&B in Leinster Square, off Westbourne.'

'I know the place. Then after the drink we'll go to Khans in Westbourne and have a meal. Indian. OK?'

'OK? Sure.'

We had one drink. I pointed out the bar's features that had not changed since the days when my parents had got together. We then walked down past the street I was born in and on to Westbourne Grove for Khans. By the time we sat we knew all about each other. I showed her my sketchbook that I carried in my inside pocket. She marvelled at the trees and nudes.

'I think drawing is the only sensible

thing I do. I am a bad father, a bad husband and a bad provider. But I draw alright.'

She looked at me with great sympathy. 'Do you feel sorry for yourself?'

'When I drink whiskey. I start like a lion and end like a whimpering lamb.'

'That should be interesting.'

'It's a spectator sport. But it's not good for the one in the ring.'

Belinda was a student passing through to Paris. She studied dance.

'How can you study dance? You either dance or you don't. Don't you mean you 'dance dance'?'

She laughed out loud.

'You really are a clever guy. You're right, I dance dance. But we have to do the studying and most of us hate it. We just want to dance.'

'It's like studying swimming. Or Art. Without doing the swimming or the art. Fuck me, what a world we live in.'

'Would you draw me?'

'I don't know about that.'

'Why?'

'Well, you know: redheads. I heard they are all rampant.'

She hit me lightly.

'Not all of us.'

'If I draw you, it's not about penetration. It's about drawing.'

'I understand that.'

'It's not a forerunner to sex, though at times it can be. But one does not necessarily lead to another.'

'Thank you for clearing up any illusions I have.'

'Let's go to your little room and let us draw that great rear of yours.'

'How do you know?'

'I know. I know by looking.'

'You have been spying on my butt?'

'I have been spying on your butt. You're got a good one for a dancer. Most dancers have no arse. Just something at the top of their legs. They might as well be boys.'

'You put it so well.'

We walked down the quiet roads off Westbourne Grove to her B&B. It had little to recommend it. We climbed three flights and we got to the small room. The place was clean but run down. She opened the door with the key and the bed dominated the room. I sat on the bed and took out my pencils. I had four and took out my small sketch book, eraser and pencil sharpener.

'How long are you in London for?'

'As I said, a few days.'

'Do you like Virginia Woolf.'

'What has that got to do with anything?'

'Just to break the tension while you revealed every last crevice of yourself to a total stranger.'

'I prefer J.D. Salinger.'

As we talked nonsense, she took off her little jacket and top. She was almost without breasts. But her figure was strong and forceful. Not as skinny as other dancers I had known. Then the turn of the denims. Her little knickers were of a particularly attractive lime green. She cast them onto the floor.

'You like green?'

'It was my mother's favourite colour. She's not with us any more. I put on green to remind me of her.'

'Green is my colour. And was my mother's colour.'

'So we have something in common. We are motherless.'

'I am fatherless, too.'

'No, I do have a dad.'

She was naked now. Her firm, strong body, with a good arse for a dancer. Her skin was white. Her nipples, like her hair, were red. Her muff hair was well shorn, but red, as red as her head of hair.

'Stand. Just stand still.'

I did a quick sketch of all of her. Then I did another and I got in close enough to smell her. Drawing someone you can smell helps. I got in so close that she loomed above me. All I could really capture was her middle, from knees to tits. I drew quickly.

'When I heard you talk, I thought you would be a fun man to know.'

'I am damaged goods. I drink too much. I have a bad temper. I am unreliable. I cope. I lost my brother recently and I feel like a piece of shit. Aside from that, I am still coping.'

'Tell us about your brother. What was his name?'

'Patrick Finbarr. He was a big blonde-haired boy. Uneducated, a drinker and smoker. But the best of fun to be with. We had more fun than with anyone. He was two years older than me. But he had a sweeter nature than mine. Mine was nasty at times. He never got nasty. He was a big dreamer. And I was always trying to get him not to dream. To be more down to earth.'

I wished that I had had water colours and drawn the light pinkish nipples, and the red wild hair. And got into the cunt and drawn the lips and the stubbles of hair where she had shorn herself, with little care. I could see her, all white and pink-red. I even imagined that we could have her in her green knickers and the combination of the lime green and pinks and reds would have made her jump off of the sheet of paper. But I just had lead pencils.

'So when do you go off?'

'I told you. I'm here a few days.'

'I must draw you with watercolours. Can I draw you tomorrow? Day or evening.'

'Don't you work?'

'I work for myself. I do what I want, largely.'

I got her to lay on the bed, with her arse turned towards me. It was slightly marked red by the pull of her knickers over her; that had left marks. As I looked at her, I realised that she was like a little piece of countryside. That she was a field, seen from a train. Undulating up to her breasts. Her muff a kind of little gulley and thicket, denuded by winter trimming.

'You made me realise that drawing women is also like drawing countryside.'

'Could you come over at 12, noon? I want to go to Oxford Street in the morning. Then we can draw all afternoon.'

'Sure.'

The idea grew in my mind. That I should look upon women as pieces of countryside. And that I might draw one woman as if I were drawing fields and hills. Remembering that at times I would look out of train windows and there would be a hill or a dell, a field with trees and clumps of trees and I would imagine that they were women. And I was looking on them as I would look on any woman.

'Can we try the knickers tomorrow? The green ones.'

She picked them up and sniffed them.

'They have to be these?'

'Yes. That green is dynamic. And with your red-pink nipples. And your red hair. Wow, it's vivid. It will wound the eye.'

She laughed.

'I like that. I'll wash them out and put the on the radiator. Just for you. Unless –.'

She went into a drawer and pulled out other knickers. They were grey, white and black. But no other greens.

'Wash the greens.'

'I'll do that.'

I drew on for another hour. She was good. We talked about Canada and why it was not America. And we talked about dancing and what she got out of it. She was going to Paris for a year on a kind of exchange. Then after the drawing she came up close to me.

'I feel as if you go now I will feel empty.'

I looked at her. I imagined, being an offensive man, or going through an offensive stage, what offensive thing could I say to her. What might a woman attracted by my offensiveness in the first place require of me? More offensiveness, I reasoned.

'I could toss you off, if you want.'

Her face looked puzzled.

'Toss me off?'

'You know, masturbate you.'

She smiled.

'No other thing on offer?'

'I am sworn for on a bible.'

'I see.'

'But a bit of finger work won't do any harm.'

She giggled.

'That's a story. I go to London. I wander by chance into a pub, and get talked into going to a boring meeting. And then I meet an offensive guy. Who takes me for an Indian meal, draws me naked. And then masturbates me.'

'There. Something you tell your grandchildren.'

She lay on back. Her legs spread apart. She was already wet.

'Can you help me with a few words.'

'What kind?'

'You know, how beautiful I am. How hot I am.'

I gave her a hard kiss on her lips. And then started to rub her cunt gently, until she gave me instruction. To rub harder and quicker. To go inside with my fingers. Her face became red and her body arched and fell, and rose again. I watched her and felt nothing; fortunately. I got a good model and she got a good bit of rubbing. Maybe tomorrow I would do the same again.

She rose into a crescendo, flailing her legs around and moaning harder and breathing harder. And then she exploded as she came, and curled herself up in a ball. I got up and threw the bed covers over her and patted her. She gave a weak little 'goodbye' and I exited. I walked down the dark worn stairs that cracked underfoot. I had known this area all my life. I was 41. I was lost in doing lots of little things. The fight against idealism would be the permanent war I would have to wage against the world. And I was an idealist who was fighting idealism. People just did not get that: that even if you were marinated in the shit thinking of idealism you still had to fight to explode the shit bubble of idealism.

I walked down to Notting Hill Gate station. I felt as if the fight against idealism might have been pushed on a few inches by my night's work: trying to demolish the cosiness of a local history club. Where people lost themselves in their petty passions while the world went down the shitter.

And the opposition to all of this idealism were themselves evil idealists. The train to Earls Court and then the train to Chiswick seemed timed for my convenience. I waited no more than a few minutes between. I thought I better wash the fish off my hands before I got into bed.

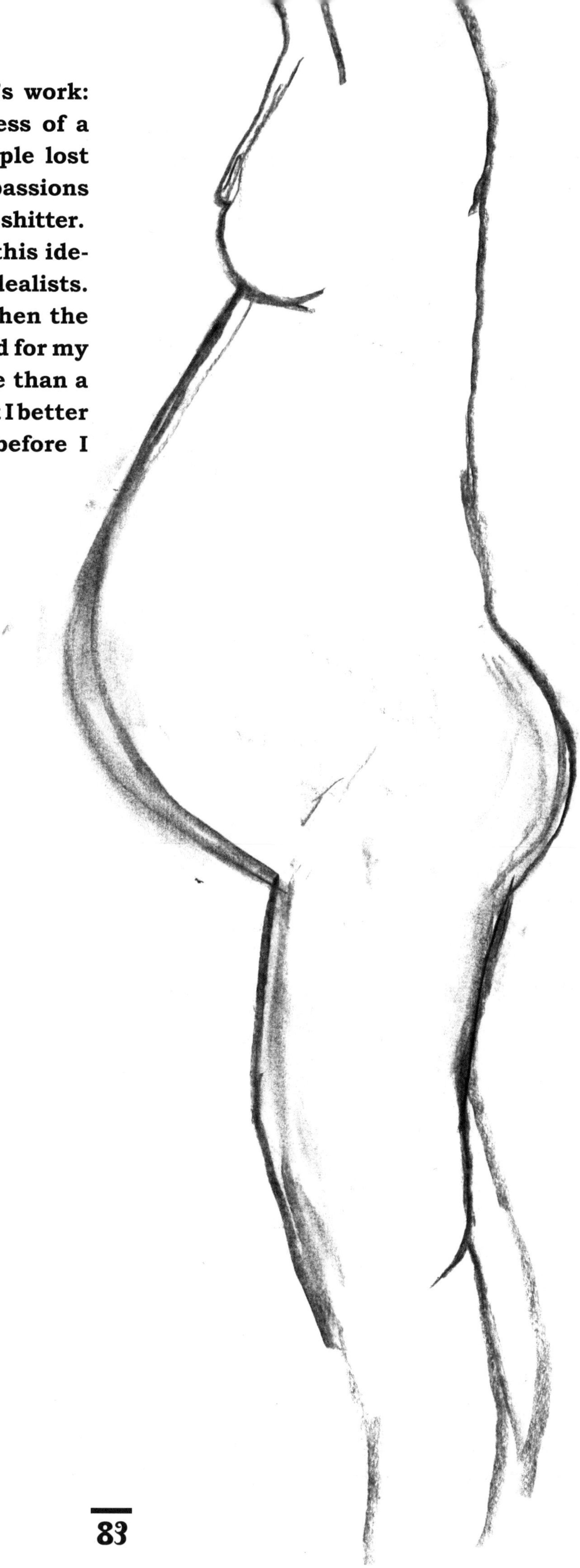

8/10/84.

Los Angeles. 1999.

I walked through the door of the large old warehouse and made my way to the drawing studio. The place was packed with drawers and the model sat almost hidden from sight by the forest of easels that surrounded her. I had my drawing bag and a large sketch book and a roll of drawing paper. A grim looking man in his 70s came up to me. He was thin and grizzled with a rough old beard and a checked shirt with a bootlace tie. He spoke as if through broken glass.

'What can I do for you, buddy?'

'I've come to draw.'

He huffed.

'Sorry, Buddy. We're easel to easel here.'

He pointed behind him.

'I saw a notice up at the big art store by the 10 Freeway exit.'

He screwed up his face and made it as nasty as he could. Considering his old riddled-with-lines face, looking as if he had been a prospector for gold in California rather than an art tutor, he did a good job of it.

'I told those motherfuckers to take that frigging sign down.'

'They didn't.'

'Obviously they didn't. But it's impossible here buddy.'

'Well, you better get that notice sorted out so you don't waste people's time. Sir.'

I went to turn.

'Come on, buddy, you can fit in somewhere. But just for tonight. Sorry about this.'

I walked around the perhaps 20 drawing people and could see there was hardly a crack for me to enter. I found a place in the end, behind the model. All I saw was her back and the chair, and her leg mostly hidden cocked up onto the arm of the chair.

Only then did I look at the model and realised I knew her. Or didn't know her. She worked in the French Café up on Abbot Kinney. I had seen her there a few times and had even tried to wish her good day, but she hardly opened her mouth to speak. I had even thought of asking her if she would join my small drawing group as a model. But she looked so superior and beautiful that she did not even bother to look at me. As this drove me on I would always make a point of wishing the best of the day and she would make some kind of noise simulating a response.

But now here she was in her great beauty. Black hair, black as a raven's wing. Good strong body with perfect tits and arse. And I was getting to draw her shoulders.

The tutor walked around and spoke to everyone before the break, with the exception of me. He came and stood behind me and then moved off after a few minutes. At break time Celestine, the model, came up to me with a big smile.

'Why, you dark horse. I did not know you were an artist.'

Her French pronunciation of English was clear and tender.

'I shall get a badge. It will say 'artist, not arsehole'.' She laughed.

'That might help. But I give you one hundred percent for persistence. You almost got me to smile. But I don't smile at work. I work. Madame does not like us to smile.'

I put out my hand.

'St. John Delarue. At your service.'

'Sinjan?'

'That is how St. John is pronounced. I am an English aristocrat.'

'Like fuck St. John. How long have you been drawing?'

'Since I was 16. I was very fortunate. I was in a reformatory for bad boys. They encouraged me to go after something. So I started to draw.'

'Encroyable. So why California?'

'Why not?

'Well, I tell you something. Now that we are friends. I am going to do a 'lay down' pose after. So I will not be on the chair. I shall be on the mattress over there. Get yourself a good place.'

I took her advice. I moved my easel over to the mattress and waited for the break to end. People talked among themselves. The tutor talked on to a few people. About President Clinton and what's a bit of spunk on a party dress anyway. Certainly not the collapse of the US political system. I watched the old goat and disliked everything about him. Celestine went round looking at people's drawings. She spoke to a few students.

I got the best position and worked hard at one drawing for the next one and a half hour session. I was pleased with what I did. I was sweating from concentration. The tutor had stood a few times behind me but said nothing. Too soon he was saying that was it and see you next week.

I got myself together, said goodbye to the model and went to pay the tutor. As I moved up, I put $25 into his hand. And gave a facetious smile.

'It was so good to be welcomed to your drawing class, sir.'

He pushed me. The force was real.

'Hang on back there, Buddy.'

He then took the money from others and after a few moments came over to me. He smiled a bad smile, showing teeth that were capped with gold. I disliked him even more.

'Hey there, Buddy. I looked at your drawings. Somewhere, back in your past you were shown how to draw. It kind of comes through. It makes itself present. But you're lazy. Your half hearted. You don't put the sweat in, except occasionally. It's a pastime for you. Some little bit of fun you can boast about, maybe. But your hand and eye are weak, except for a few moments, a few pieces. You need to work on it. You're always welcome here. But you better get here early. Otherwise it's backs and nothing else. Get here early. You can draw, but you've gotta frigging work at it.'

I was astonished He had complimented me and insulted me. If I worked hard I might get someone. But I was lazy. Skilled, maybe even talented, but lazy. I stood looking at him, completely thrown by the experience.

'So I'm in?'

'You're in. But you've gotta work. These others are slappers. They slap their pencils about like soft dicks. You can draw. But you've got to draw in order to draw. There is no alternative. It can't be talked about. It has to be drawn. Come up to my place in Topanga on Saturday. That'll be crowded. Say, d'you wanna have a drink with me and my lady and Celestine?'

'I'm going to eat at the Broadway Deli in Santa Monica.'

'We'll join you there.'

He shook my hand. It was one of the

hardest hands I had ever held. And from a man as thin as a pipe cleaner. And a grizzled face like a 49'er, from the Californian gold rush.

I drove to Santa Monica and parked up the car in the structure opposite the Broadway Deli. I had been in LA six months and was doing a bit of drawing. I had formed LAADD with a woman and a few friends. We drew in my small studio in Marina Del Rey, a few miles down the ocean. I was on the Speedway, with the ocean and the sand just behind the house. I could hear it at times breaking on the beach. Everything was sun and sea and sand. And in the daytime I drove to Downtown to talk with people who were homeless and looking for work. And went to meetings with officials about giving work to the needy.

LAADD: Los Angeles Academy of Drinking and Drawing. But my fellow drawers and models were not always available. They travelled off. They had other things to do. I was reduced to drawing myself in a mirror, out on my small balcony. And drawing the palm trees that stood by the balcony, as if poking their noses into my small studio. Sometimes the four of us slept over, two above and two below in a big blue double bunk bed I had bought at a knock down price on Lincoln Boulevard. I was settling in. I could live here forever because LA felt timeless.

The only fly in the ointment was a woman I pursued; only by spanking her could I get her attention. Soon there would be a movie called The Secretary to explain the condition of her mind. But I understood nothing before that movie lifted the scales from my eyes.

The maitre d' led me to a booth as I said there would be four of us. The booth was under the control of a waitress who for six months I had been polite to. And she had ignored me. Not so much as a smile, though smiles were handed out to all and sundry. This night she looked annoyed at the sight of one person taking a four-person booth and it was only on being told that I was to be joined by three others that she took her off face and put on a civil, though distant one. I sat and ordered a glass of wine and a glass of water and she went off. I took out a small sketchbook and started looking at a few small sketches I had made that night. She came back with the wine and water. Putting the small tray down she knocked the sketchbook off the table. She scrambled to pick it up. It had fallen open. Instead of handing it straight back to me she looked at the opened sketch.

'D'you mind?'

'Go ahead.'

She flicked through some of the other sketches and her face changed to something I had not seen in all the months I had been coming into the Deli. It was interest. I watched her face. She stood looking deeply at the pages, each one throwing up a kind of modification of 'interest'. After a few minutes, she turned her face to engage mine.

'These look good.'

She smiled.

'Thank you.'

It seemed as though in California no one knew you until they got a handle on you. If you dressed well, or noticeably; if you were stylish, you were noticed.

Or young and beautiful. But to Celestine at the Café, only when she saw me drawing did she bother to recognise I was there. And now the waitress, who had overlooked my friendliness now had a handle on me. I was a person who drew naked women. That put me above the hoard who came in to the Deli and did not have money oozing from them; or who probably were not connected to the film industry. I was an artist.

She put the book down and went off. When she came back with the menu her whole face was changed. I was changed. I realised that now I had made the equivalent of an LA friend. That I might now be included. That I had gone from being the background to being in the foreground. Did this do something for my soul? I certainly felt not being ignored was good for something.

She did not need to come back a third time but she did. She stood above me. Tall, blonde, well made with a good arse. And now a good smile.

'Do you, do you draw people who are not models?'

She was embarrassed. It was good to see this good-looking woman embarrassed after she had given me so much discomfort for all the time I came into the deli. I knew if I fell into her area I would enjoy the eating experience and the social time less than with other waitresses. She was the ogre I would prefer not to have to try break. But now she stood above me.

'I would love to draw you Madge.'

She went red, and for a moment sat down at the booth. You only did that on rare occasions. The management did not approve of waitresses sitting down with the clients, though occasionally if it was an important person you were allowed.

'Thank you. Can I meet you for a coffee. I have always wanted to be drawn.'

'Drawing is good for the soul.'

'I believe it. For the drawer and the drawn.'

She put it well enough. How many people who went round with a face like a smacked arse in LA were really waiting to be drawn? All I had to do was get them naked and soon enough they would opening up like flowers deprived of water.

We arranged to meet at Chez Jay's after her shift. There was more than likely to be a few stars there. Or potential stars. We met. Madge was a star in the making, or in waiting. A few days later she came to my new apartment off Main Street where Venice met Santa Monica. Right on the ocean. I was four blocks from the ocean. I gave her a robe and she went into the bathroom and came out in the robe. As was the decent method, the protocol. When she took off the robe I saw a woman who was strong and big breasted, and good arsed. With a red face. And an embarrassed smile.

'Yes, drawing naked women is good for the soul.'

'I hope so. Sometimes I feel I need a soul.'

And then we began. And each week for four hours we would meet in my apartment near the ocean and I would draw her. I gave her the best drawings. We talked a lot. We became friends, in an LA way. But I realised that she was, as she said, looking for a soul. Connecting

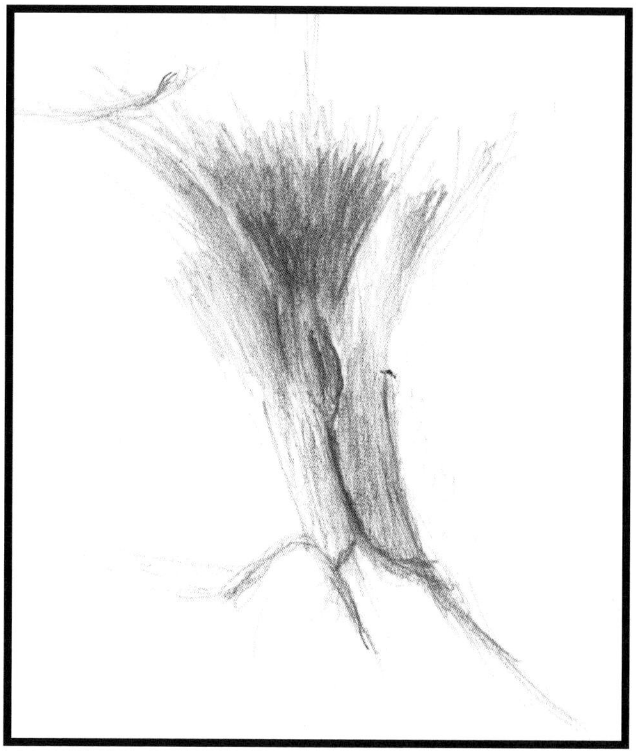

to something that the saunas and masseurs and the beauticians could not give her. I was adding to the layers of herself. I was enriching her life, and hopefully enriching her depth; and the promise of depth was what all movie stars needed. They thirsted after it. Madge was after it, so maybe it might make a change, a frisson of depth that could be grasped by the people who auditioned her.

She got a few jobs. She was away for a while and the sessions stopped. It was good for my soul and I felt it might have given Madge a soul that she sorely needed. In the way that Marilyn Monroe desperately desired one. Soul meaning depth: challenging the facia of body and appearance. She wanted to have depths. And Madge, 40 years after Marilyn was also desiring a soul. I helped build Madge's soul for her.

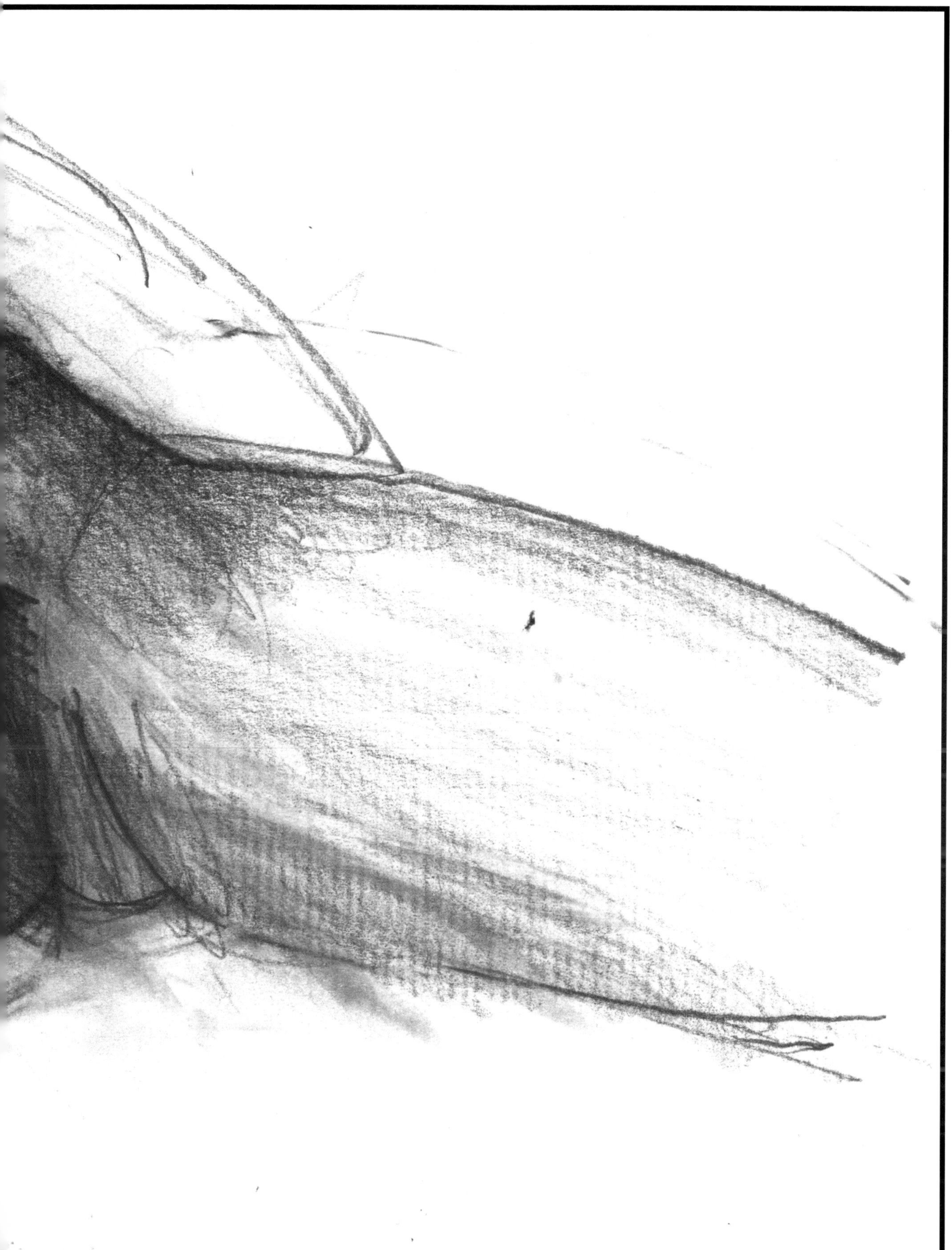

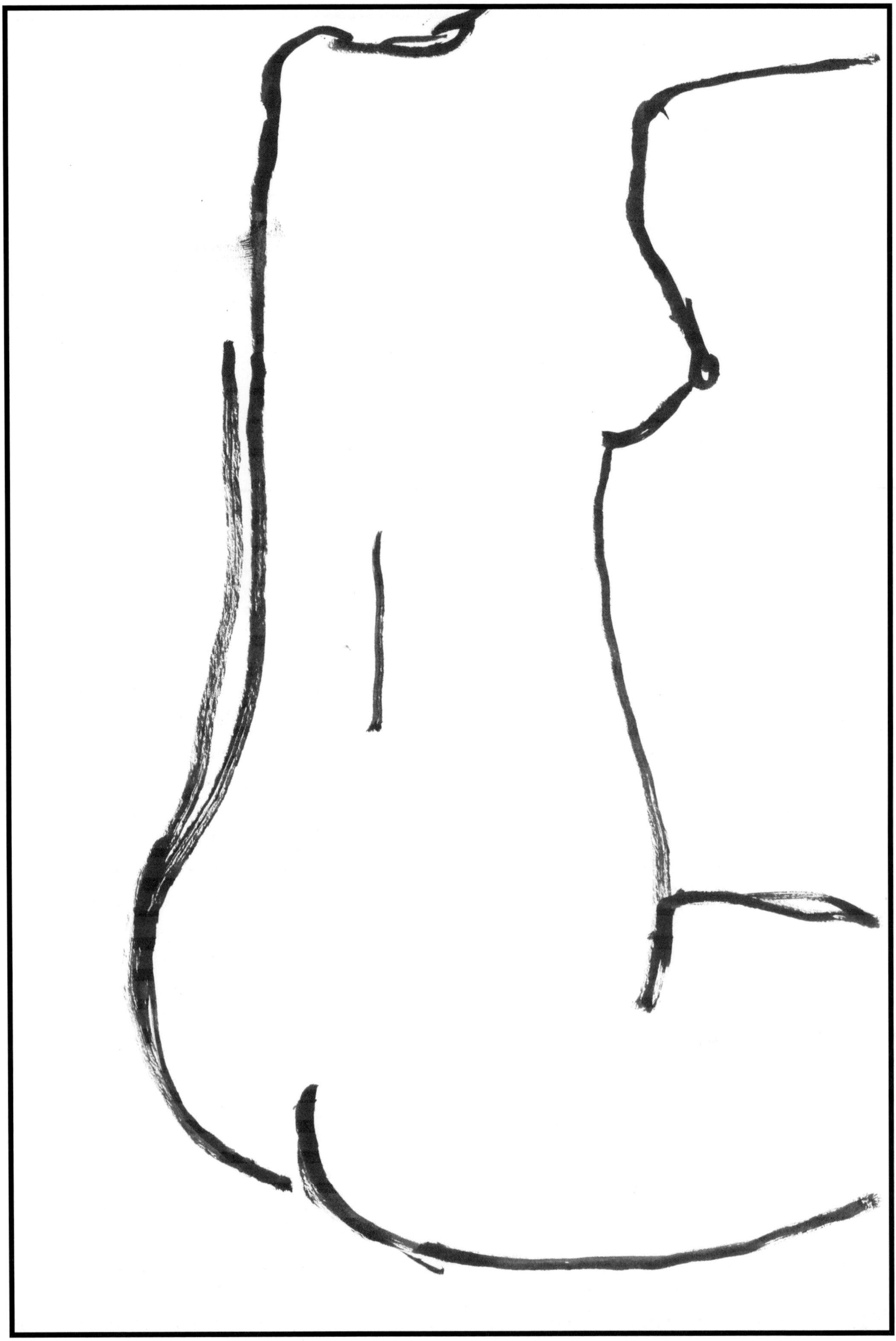

Marylebone. 2003.

The revolutionary postman delivered to me that morning. He ran the bell and was waiting on the wet doorstep for me, stamping his feet. I opened the door too late; you could tell it on his face.

'I was going to leave you a card.'

'I was putting on my trousers.'

He made me sign for the small package. I had never met a postman as miserable as this man. And I knew him. I knew him from the 1970s. But he had such a suffering face, a suffering look to him so I dared not try and remind him of the times we knew each other.

He moved away and then stopped. He turned around and looked at me as I looked at the small package.

'We know each other.'

I looked up at him.

'We did. We were in the revolutionary Party together. Destroying Capitalism.'

He walked back.

'What a pile of shit that was.'

He had long lank grey hair, a beard, unlike the clean cut revolutionary he was then.

'You were a lecturer I believe. At London University or something. An intellectual.'

'And then I was told to go and work in a factory. So I worked in factories. Turned my back on education and privilege. And then the tide turned and I was fucked. In the proletariat while others went on and went their own way.'

He looked at me accusingly.

'So now you are a postman.'

'A temporary postman. I have been a temporary postman for nearly two years. And you? Property owner in Marylebone. You must have done well for yourself.'

'I rent. This is not my flat.'

He looked cunningly, or what he thought was cunningly.

'But come on, you've done well. You're probably very comfortable.'

'I rent. I may have done well. I started in the underclass. I got to the middle class. You have gone the other way.'

'Tell me about it.'

'Would you like to come in for a tea.'

He laughed.

'I am working. This isn't some social thing with me.'

He turned and walked away. He saw me as one who had done well out of revolutionary politics. Someone who had made a career. That's why he was so sour, I reasoned. An educated member of the middle classes who got sent into factories to convince workers to take up the revolutionary party's programme. And then got left and presumably couldn't get back into the middle class world of education.

The small package was a book. I felt it. It said 'not to be opened until the big day'. The big day was a week away. My birthday. I looked at the stamp. It was from Holland. It was from the multi millionaire who always sent me a little present for my birthday. One year it was a watch that ticked and tocked for about a week. I went out in the rain and the watch got wet and it worked no more. Another time it was a small bottle of stuff you rubbed on your hands when there was no water around. You used it presumably when you went for a shit in the woods and you could not use water, having used leaves to clean your arse. Another time it was a very large handkerchief with an ancient map of the world on it, a nautical map with Neptune blowing winds form his mouth.

It always occurred to me that the multi millionaire was taking the piss out of me. That he could have bought me a Ferrari with his small change but chose not to. And why should he? He owed me nothing. We were supposed friends. And I was not likely to share in his largesse because that was not the way. Or the way that he had set it up between us.

I was a highly amusing, funny, committed piece of floor show. A joy to be with who made him and his girlfriend laugh hysterically with my drive, energy and humour. And he looked on and like a medieval king was pleased enough to send me a shitty little gift.

I watched the postman through the window. Perhaps I should invite him in for a tea another time. And we could talk about revolutionary times and climes. And how we were going to tear down Capitalism and replace it with Socialism.

I tidied the front room and got out my drawing materials. I took the easel from the back room and set it up in the front room. Just as I got the last of the paper and charcoal the door bell rang and I buzzed in Ellie. She came in and kissed me lightly on the cheek.

'Tea?'

She went into the kitchen and started filling the kettle.

'Just yourself. I've had enough tea.'

I turned up the fire heater. It was a cold day but Ellie seemed impervious to the cold. She made her tea. We talked about her flatmates and a boy she liked. And then she went into the bathroom to change. And I sat and waited for the fair-haired architecture student with bright blue eyes to return to pose. She came in and took off her gown, and there she stood. I quickly drew a few standing poses, one a minute, to loosen up my hand. And then she sat and I started to draw her arse with great care. I wanted to publish postcards of my various carefully drawn arses. And the occasional quick sketch with charcoal. Ellie was talkative so I listened to her story about her flatmates and the boy as I drew carefully with a well-sharpened pencil. An hour passed quickly and then another hour and Ellie had to leave for her Saturday afternoon job. I paid her. We lightly kissed and I looked at this fine girl and thanked the friend for introducing us.

I took a bath, dressed and it was 2pm and Sophie came to clean the flat. I would walk around and spend two hours at the Wallace Collection, looking at the works of Francois Boucher, as I did most Saturdays that Sophie cleaned. She had cleaned the flat before I came and she asked that I continue the arrangement. I did, paying her the same money as she got before. Then one day she asked for another pound an hour and I gave it to her. She looked at me with a concerned crease on her brow.

'Why you just pay? Lady upstairs, she argue.'

'I am not the lady upstairs.'

'But she got big beautiful place. Money hanging on wall. You have Ikea.'

‘Two pounds is not the end of the world.’

This puzzled her.

‘Not end of world? Explain.’

So I stopped and told her it meant that the money would not break my fortunes. She smiled.

‘I like this.’

Today I rushed out and went straight to the Wallace Collection. Living in the centre of London had many advantages. The Wallace collection was one of the reasons why I moved from Brixton Hill in the south into the centre of London. I drew most of the afternoon at the gallery, and then went back to pay Sophie; and then remembered as I got near to the door that I had not taken down the drawings of Ellie. Usually I took them down and rolled them up and put them in the back room. So as not to offend Sophie. But when I went in the front room was cleaned and the drawings were stuck on the walls. I started to take them down. Sophie came in with a sheepish smile.

‘You do this?’

‘Yes. I have a model Saturday morning before you come. I am sorry. I forgot to take them down.’

She looked at them.

‘Good. I see that. How much you pay the model?’

I told her. Her face went rather red.

‘More than me?’

‘The rate is set by art schools. That is the rate you pay.’

When Sophie first came I would often stay in the flat. She had jet black hair and I would watch her move around. She was probably in her late 20s. She had some indentations on her face from what might have been an accident. But overall she was good looking, strong. At times she would crouch down and I would see the crevice of her buttocks. That is why I started to go out and not stay in. And then I realised that my politeness was good and that going to the Wallace Collection for those two hours was a continuation of my education and my chance to draw.

I had not seen Sophie annoyed in the six months since I moved in and she cleaned.

‘Cleaning is harder than laying still.’

‘I bet it is.’

‘No. It is. I lay still at college for art. For a few years. I know how to lay still. But cleaning harder.’

I could not help smile.

‘So you have posed?’

‘Of course!’

She then went off to carry on cleaning. She was very thorough. I found her in the bathroom, bending down, showing her crevice.

‘Sophie, the girl I draw, will end in a few weeks.’

She stood up and turned around.

‘No more drawing?’

‘No more drawing of her.’

She looked at me carefully.

‘Maybe then I become model.’

‘Could you clean and model?’

She smiled.

‘Be good! Yes. Two hours and two hours.’

‘Yes?’

She took off a yellow plastic glove and shook my hand.

‘When? Now?’

‘Why not.’

‘But must finish first.’

She carried on cleaning for another twenty minutes and then she had a cup of tea. And she sat on the sofa and started to talk about the people she had posed for. But then she had moved from Bristol to London and her modelling ended. I watched her and felt good that soon I would be drawing her. We drank more tea, and I gave her a piece of cake. Then she stood and went into the bathroom. She came out in the gown that earlier Ellie had worn. She had a smile on her face.

'My body more interesting than my cleaning.'

She took off the gown in the front room in front of the gas fire. And stood and looked at me admiring her. Her white skin with the usual lighter colour around the bikini area. The big strong buttocks. She turned so that I could see her. Her smile seemed frozen on her face. Her breasts free of all constraints.

I looked at her and realised she was right. Her cleaning was good, very good. But she seemed to have a figure from the old days. Big and strong, like an Italian movie star of the 1950s. The kind of girl's body I grew up on, never liking the boyishness of English girls of the 60s.

'Want me which way?'

'Just standing.'

I then noticed that she had put on her lipstick, something she normally reserved for her last moments in the flat before she walked out into the street. The red was 1950s Italian Movie Star Red.

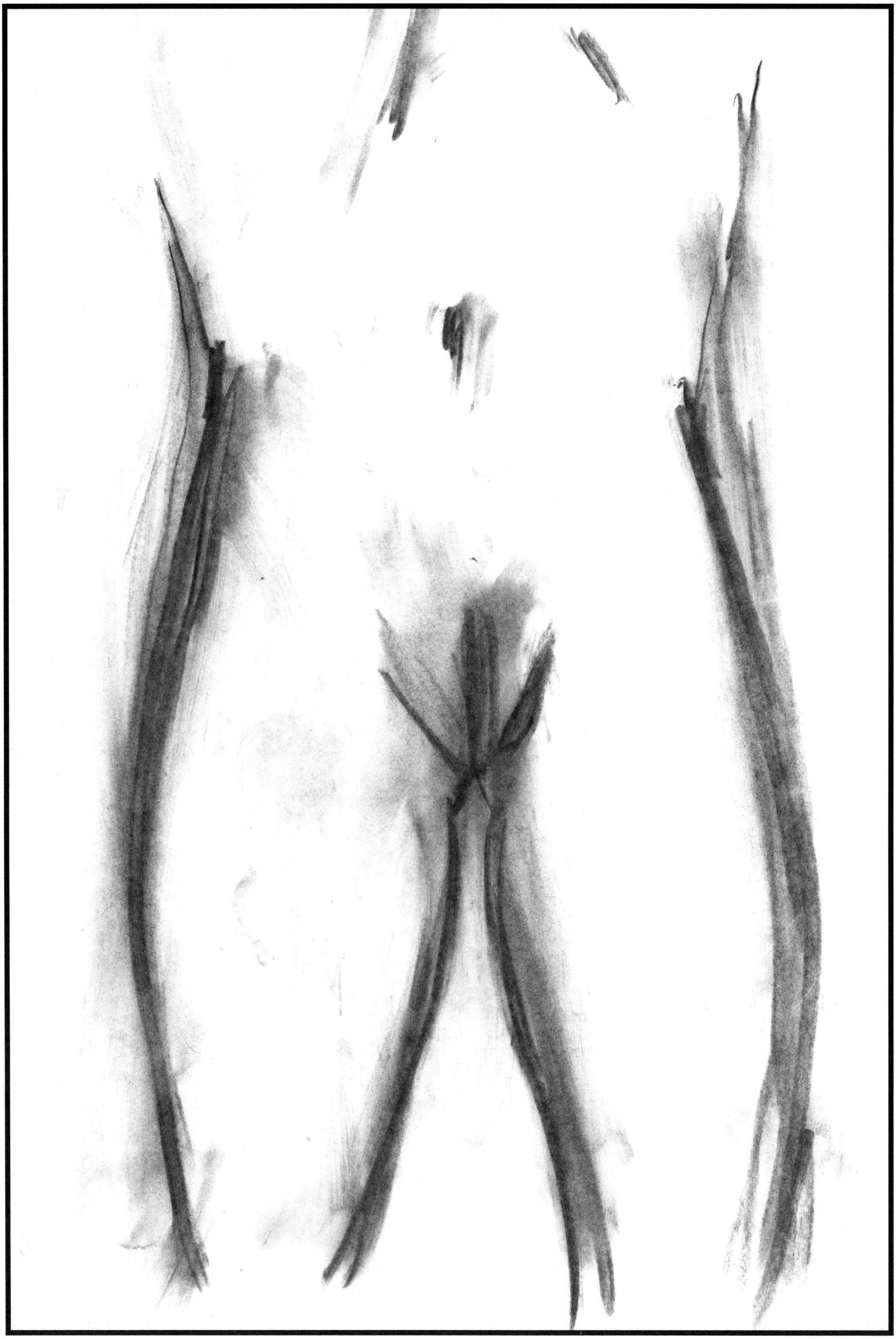

Exposure, Notting Hill, Two. 2013.

The talk was well received. The projections of naked women onto the walls had been overwhelming. One or two particular drawings I had done, projected so large, made me look better than I was. A few stain-like drawings worked particularly well. The eyes of a model I had met in Paris blazed out, even though they were little more than stains upon the paper. But blown up, they made her eyes look strangely powerful.

I left the stage of the event feeling good about my work. I sold many books, which I signed. I sold some posters of the exhibition I had had the year before. This was all good stuff. But it was all too nice. It wasn't the niceness that had got me drawing in the first place. I was a badly made boy and I felt that if I wrote stories it would show the nasty life out of which grew my drawing.

As I left the theatre a woman with an accent came up to me and half whispered:

'You fucking fraud. You fucking demagogue. Like Hitler, you were fucked in the head at childhood.'

'Did I talk like a demagogue?'

'You talked as if you were some superior life. Fuck you! Many people have had a worse life than you.'

'Why did you stay? If it was so much shit.'

'I paid ten pound, wasted listening to your self-opinionated rubbish.'

'What about the drawings?'

'Huff! The drawings was only an excuse to get women's knickers down. And all these people stupidly fell for it.'

'Are you Austrian?'

'That is no business of yours.'

She sounded like an Austrian woman I met a few years before who had harangued me along the same lines. Who likewise had used the Hitler link. Was this another Austrian?

I smiled. She could not appreciate how she brought me back to the bad and nasty place out of which my drawings came. I laughed and wanted to embrace her, but she would not be embraced. Her boyfriend got involved and tried to push me away. But I side stepped him and he stumbled and fell. And then they were off in the crowd, as she pulled him from the fucked-up man who had used his drawing of naked women to get some 'fucked-upness' out of himself.

The talk had taken place around the corner from where I was born in Notting Hill. Being back minutes from my place of nativity seemed appropriate. The streets I had played in as a ragged boy living a violent, hungry slum life. Out of which eventually I managed to understand a thing or two. As I said to a brother once: that I had made the most of adversity and used art to get into the middle classes. I stood in the bar and talked to a number of people, all of them saying that it was good to see art put to such good use. I left early because I needed more grit. I needed more people around me who doubted my sincerity. They encouraged me to think. Too many agree-ers seemed dull and boring.

We are all Picasso until we are 10, maybe11. And then we are in recovery. The talk was useful because it was the first time I had ever really explained the importance of my drawing as a means of socialisation.

Back at home I carried on reading a new book about Churchill. And wondered when my day would come. When I would be called out of a wasted life to do useful things. And fell asleep in the armchair.